ABIDING
ASTONISHMENT

LITERARY CURRENTS IN BIBLICAL INTERPRETATION

EDITORS

Danna Nolan Fewell
Perkins School of Theology,
Southern Methodist University, Dallas TX
David M. Gunn
Columbia Theological Seminary, Decatur GA

EDITORIAL ADVISORY BOARD

Jack Dean Kingsbury
Union Theological Seminary in Virginia, Richmond VA
Peter D. Miscall
St Thomas Seminary, Denver CO
Gary A. Phillips
College of the Holy Cross, Worcester MA
Regina M. Schwartz
Department of English, Duke University, Durham NC
Mary Ann Tolbert
The Divinity School, Vanderbilt University, Nashville TN

ABIDING ASTONISHMENT

---

psalms, modernity, and the making of history

WALTER BRUEGGEMANN

•

WESTMINSTER/JOHN KNOX PRESS
Louisville, Kentucky

ABIDING ASTONISHMENT:
PSALMS, MODERNITY, AND THE MAKING OF HISTORY

© 1991 Walter Brueggemann

First edition

Published by Westminster/John Knox Press,
Louisville, Kentucky

Library of Congress Cataloging-in-Publication Data

Brueggemann, Walter.
  Abiding Astonishment : Psalms, modernity, and the making of history
/ Walter Brueggemann. — 1st ed.
    p.   cm. — (Literary currents in biblical interpretation)
  Includes bibliographical references and indexes.
  ISBN 0-664-25134-X

  1. Bible. O.T. Psalms—Criticism, interpretation, etc.
I. Title. II. Series.
BS1430.2.B779 1991
223'.206—dc20   91-260

CONTENTS

SERIES
PREFACE

New currents in biblical interpretation are emerging. Questions about origins—authors, intentions, settings—and stages of composition are giving way to questions about the literary qualities of the Bible, the play of its language, the coherence of its final form, and the relations between text and readers.

Such literary criticism is rapidly acquiring sophistication as it learns from major developments in secular critical theory, especially in understanding the instability of language and the key role of readers in the production of meaning. Biblical critics are being called to recognize that a plurality of readings is an inevitable and legitimate consequence of the interpretive process. By the same token, interpreters are being challenged to take responsibility for the theological, social, and ethical implications of their readings.

Biblical interpretation is changing on the practical as well as the theoretical level. More readers, both inside and outside the academic guild, are discovering that the Bible in literary perspective can powerfully engage people's lives. Communities of faith where the Bible is foundational may find that literary criticism can make the Scripture accessible in a way that historical criticism seems unable to do.

Within these changes lie exciting opportunities for all who seek contemporary meaning in the ancient texts. The goal of the series is to encourage such change and such search, to breach the confines of traditional biblical criticism, and to open channels for new currents of interpretation.

—THE EDITORS

PREFACE

This brief manuscript is a quite personal attempt to sort out for myself some categories of interpretation. Its conclusions are in the same way quite personal conclusions about what I have thought, how I interpret our present situation *vis à vis* the text, and how I intend to proceed in my work. The questions I have addressed were not assigned to me, nor was I invited to write or speak on them, nor indeed, have I checked them out anywhere very much. For all of the personal nature of such reflection, however, scholarship is relentlessly and inevitably a public process. For that reason I am glad to share what I have thought, even glad, with appropriate trepidation, to submit my thinking for critical response. I regard what I have done as provisional as well as personal. It certainly is not any final conclusion. Still, I hope it is a useful step along the way.

My reflection which culminates in this manuscript has been given impetus by three factors. First, on October 30, 1986, I presented the Leo Dehon Lecture at Sacred Heart School of Theology in Hales Corners, Wisconsin. The topic assigned was "the Historical Psalms." I enjoyed the hospitality of the seminary and was graciously hosted by Professor Joseph R. Dean, SCJ. I had never much thought about the historical Psalms before, so that the invitation provided an opportunity for fresh reflection. Second, in 1987 I enjoyed the leisure of a sabbatical year in Cambridge, supported by Eden Theological Seminary and Columbia Theological Seminary. I benefitted greatly from a bibliography shared with me by David Jobling (most of which I read carefully) concerning the interface between theories of textuality and sociological analysis. The results of that reading are evident here and my debt to Jobling is considerable. Third, my return from sabbatical and fresh immersion in seminary education and in the life of the church have led me to recognize that the interpretive crisis in the Euro-American Church is much deeper than I had thought. It is a crisis that cannot be covered over either by "objective criticism" or by shrill scholastic theology. I have in the end been concerned not with how these texts function in a community which trusts them, but how they function with freedom and disturbing power. My own thinking and this manuscript have evolved greatly since my initial presentation at Sacred Heart School of Theology. It is clear that I am profoundly dependent upon the very scholars whose perspectives I critique. My borrowing, and therefore my debts, are very large. That, in any case, is how scholarship works. In the end, caught as we are, somewhere between modernity and marginality, my urging is toward more self-critical intentionality, so that we become more aware than we have been of our stake in, and benefit from, our interpretive posture.

It is evident that I continue to be indebted to the programmatic work of Norman Gottwald, and to George Lindbeck's concern for language as decisive for community. I am grateful to Davis Perkins for his willingness to take on this piece in his new work at Westminster/John Knox, and to Danna Nolan Fewell and my colleague David M. Gunn for including it in their new series. I am daily grateful to Tempie Alexander who, though she did not work extensively on this manuscript, attended to much else in the meantime so that I could complete my work on it. Finally, I am, as so often, grateful to Donna Lograsso for her patience, care, expertise, and good spirit in typing this manuscript.

In referring to the biblical text, I have followed the New Revised Standard Version, except where I have made adjustments to utilize inclusive language.

It is my hope that the church (along with the synagogue) will continue to think again and think hard about the text entrusted to us, about how we host this text, and that occasionally we will let it have its dangerous say among us. With recent events in Eastern Europe, none of us can fail to see that a truth-telling text can indeed have a power for newness all its own, without consorting with either established modes of knowledge or established modes of power. It is undeniable that this biblical text, in all its canonical splendor, is the provocateur of many other dangerous texts that have come in its wake.

—WALTER BRUEGGEMANN
Columbia Theological Seminary   July 9, 1990

ABIDING
ASTONISHMENT

INTRODUCTION

RECITING
HISTORY

To read the "historical Psalms" (Psalms 78, 105, 106, 136) is to confront vexed problems of history, historicity, and historiography. Yet these Psalms are also characteristically treated in Old Testament scholarship as Psalms of historical *recital*, a rubric which immediately shifts our attention to speech, rhetoric, communication, and eventually literature. Thus in discussing the "the recital of the historical Psalms," we find ourselves in the interface between "what happened" (history) on the one hand, and "what is remembered" and "how it is said" (rhetoric) on the other. Indeed, "*what* happened" turns out to be dependent upon and determined by *how* the happenedness is shaped in the speech practices of the remembering community.[1]

It is now a truism in Old Testament studies to say that we are making a methodological turn away from "historical" to "literary" studies.[2] It is agreed by most scholars that these approaches and methods are interrelated and both have a role to play. The dispute, however, turns on the relative importance of each method and the methodological beginning point. This study of "historical Psalms" does not assume, as almost no one assumes, that the Psalms are "records" of what happened. They are rather, as all historical remembering is, rhetorical acts which shape the past in certain ways, and which deny or exclude other shapings of the past. Moreover, we now know, even in scripture study, that rhetorical acts are never innocent or neutral acts, but are always partisan acts reflective of vested interest that may be hidden or overt. It is not denied that somewhere in these recitals there are "factual" events, but the notion of "factual" already begins to distort (in the interest of imagined objectivity) the inevitable power of rhetoric and the inescapable authority of interest in every rendering of the past. Thus in the notion of the "recital of the historical Psalms," our emphasis will fall on "recital," for it is the recital that generates the "happenedness"; and every recital chooses some "happenedness" and rejects others. Both the formation and the continued use of these Psalms, I shall argue, mediated Israel's remembered past to Israel's present in particular ways. Thus "history" is in every instance a chosen mode of rhetoric.[3] This is as true of modern "descriptions" which purport to be "objective," but which rely upon constructive acts of imagination,"[4] as it is of the ancient recitals which are admittedly "theological." In the continued reference to and use of these Psalms in the church and synagogue, we are participants in a specific practice of rhetoric which is a particular form of power. I shall argue in what follows that such rhetoric and power have important present-tense significance for the community which refers to these texts, present-tense significance which can cut more than one way.

I

THE
PSALMS
OF
HISTORICAL
RECITAL

Under the influence of Gerhard von Rad (and George Ernest Wright), Old Testament scholarship has for two generations focused its interpretive work on "the recital of God's mighty deeds."[5] The hypothesis of the "credo recital" has exercised an enormous influence. This hypothesis suggests that from a core memory of "Exodus-reception of the land" (cf. Deut 6:20-24; 26:5-9; Josh 24:1-13),[6] the Old Testament has, through a long process of reiterated recital, expanded the memory so that the recital shapes and structures the entire Hexateuch.

That hypothesis has more recently been seriously criticized and much doubted. It is doubted on *historical-critical grounds*, because the texts upon which von Rad based his work are now thought not to be early, and so cannot be the source of Israel's historical recital. More seriously, the hypothesis is regarded as problematic on *hermeneutical grounds*, because the notion that "God acts in history" has been shown to be difficult and ambiguous.[7] The phrase constitutes an unsorted mixing of theological and historical categories.[8] Moreover von Rad was never able to clarify what is "scientific history" and what is "salvation history," and how the two are related.[9]

Having acknowledged the current criticisms of von Rad's hypothesis, in this discussion I want to pursue one aspect of von Rad's general argument, namely the problems and possibilities for "history" in the Psalms of "historical recital."[10] The pertinent Psalms are 78, 105, 106, and 136, though other Psalms might derivatively be included.[11] Von Rad simply comments that these poetic statements follow "the canonical outline," and that these several Psalms variously included or excluded elements of the canonical recital.[12] It may indeed be possible to suggest specific contexts and dates for these several Psalms on the basis of what is included in or excluded from them. That, however, is not my concern here. The four Psalms (78, 105, 106, 136) belong together in terms of their content and style of presentation. It is immediately clear, however, that these Psalms express very different theological points, meet very different liturgical needs, and serve very different social-liturgical functions.

A summary of the communal needs and social functions reflected in and served by these Psalms includes the following:

1. Psalm 105 is a glad, unqualified celebration of God's gracious deeds, with a particular focus on the gift of the land. In verses 8-10, there is a double reference to covenant and the oath of Yahweh, which leads to a discernment of land as an "inheritance" (vs. 11).

> God is mindful of the covenant forever,
>> of the word commanded for a thousand generations,
> the covenant which God made with Abraham,
>> God's sworn promise to Isaac,
> confirmed to Jacob as a statute,
>> to Israel as an everlasting covenant,
> saying, "to you I will give the land of Canaan
>> as your portion for an inheritance." (vss. 8-11)

The reference to God's promise is reiterated in verse 42, implicitly a promise of the land, and again in verses 43-44, where the people gladly enter the "lands" of the nations (pl.):

> For God remembered the holy promise,
>> and Abraham, God's servant.

16

So God brought out this people with joy,
>   the chosen ones with singing.
And God gave them the lands of the nations;
>   and they took possession of the wealth of the peoples
>   . . . . (vss. 42-44)

The hinge of the Psalm appears to be in the last verse:

to the end that [ba'avur] they should keep God's statutes,
>   and observe God's laws. (vs. 45)[13]

The entire Psalm provides a basis for the *embrace of obedience* in verse 45, an obedience which is untroubled and uncontested. This Psalm reflects a situation of theological "innocence" in Israel's trust of Yahweh. The recital of the memory is an invitation to be obedient to the God of the covenant who makes promises and who keeps them.[14]

2. Psalm 106 is a complete contrast to Psalm 105. The same normative historical memory is now turned to become a recital of Israel's sin, failure, and recalcitrance. The great deeds of Yahweh are characteristically refused and rejected. This resistance on Israel's part regularly foils Yahweh's resolve to give good gifts. The Psalm contrasts the recalcitrance of Israel against the fidelity of Yahweh:

Nevertheless God regarded their distress,
>   upon hearing their cry.
God remembered for their sake the covenant,
>   and relented according to the abundance of God's
>   steadfast love.
God caused them to be pitied
>   by all those who held them captive. (vss. 44-5)

The Psalm culminates in verse 47 with an appeal that Yahweh should rescue and gather Israel, presumably from exile:

Save us, O Lord our God,
>   and gather us from among the nations,
that we may give thanks to thy holy name
>   and glory in thy praise. (vs. 47)

The purpose of the negative recital is *to mount a petition.* The ground of the petition for rescue is that disobedient Israel has no recourse but to rely on Yahweh's gracious fidelity. (The negative recital in this Psalm, focusing on Israel's unfaithfulness, reflects a trajectory in Israel's poetry that runs from Deuteronomy 32 to the late petitions of Ezra 9, Nehemiah 9, and Daniel 9.)

3. Psalm 136 is highly stylized and exhibits the recital of "mighty deeds" now embedded in a fixed liturgic antiphon. After every verse of the normative recital, the congregation answers, "For God's steadfast love endures forever." This Psalm is in some way instructional, showing that the general conviction of God's fidelity (the main point of the recital) is constituted by quite concrete and identifiable memories.[15] The Psalm begins and ends (vss. 1-3, 26) with a summons to thank, suggesting that Israel's entire life of recital is encompassed in a comprehensive mood and act of *gratitude:*

O give thanks to the Lord, for God is good,
> for God's steadfast love endures for ever.
O give thanks to the God of gods,
> for God's steadfast love endures for ever.
O give thanks to the Lord of lords,
> for God's steadfast love endures forever . . .
O give thanks to the God of heaven,
> for God's steadfast love endures for ever. (vss. 1-3, 26)

Israel's normative response to Yahweh's rescuing fidelity is one of praise and gratitude. Gratitude (*hodu*) sets the perimeters of Israel's life with God, and there is in Israel a great deal for which to be grateful. Gratitude stands at the beginning and end of all of Israel's life, as at the beginning and end of this Psalm.

4. Psalm 78 is very different from the other three Psalms we have mentioned and perhaps the most interesting. It shares with Psalm 106 the sense of Israel's repeated failure in covenant through sin, rebellion, and recalcitrance:

They did not keep God's covenant,
>   but refused to walk according to God's law.
They forgot what God had done,
>   and the miracles that God had shown them.
>   (vss. 10-11; cf. 17-8, 32, 36-7, 40, 56-8)

This Psalm underscores Israel's decisive sin in two ways. First, the Psalm dares to assert that Israel's sin is so serious that Yahweh "utterly rejects" (*me'as me'od*) them (vs. 59). Second, this harsh theological judgment that Yahweh may terminate covenant with Israel is not a politically disinterested statement.[16] The phrase "utterly rejects" (culminating in vs. 67) does not suggest that Yahweh is finished entirely with this people, however, but only with the northern political arrangement organized around Saul and its northern priestly apparatus of Shiloh. The God who has "utterly rejected" has also "chosen" (vss. 68-72). According to the recital, God has displaced the power arrangements of the old covenant community and has authorized the new royal-temple apparatus of Jerusalem. While this Psalm appeals to the old covenantal realities, it clearly has a different focus.

Clearly, the theological contrast between destroyed Shiloh (vs. 60) and newly chosen Jerusalem is politically useful for the legitimacy of Jerusalem:

God abandoned God's own dwelling at Shiloh,
>   the tent where God dwelt among mortals . . .
but God chose the tribe of Judah,
>   Mount Zion, which God loves.
God built God's own sanctuary like the high heavens,
>   like the earth, which God has founded for ever.
God chose David as servant,
>   and took him from the sheepfolds;
from tending the nursing ewes God brought him
>   to be shepherd of God's own people,
>   of Israel, God's inheritance. (vss. 60, 68-71)

In Jer 7:12-15, in a later generation, the prophet makes a more difficult and dangerous argument:

Go now to my place that was in Shiloh, where I made my name dwell at first, and see what I did to it for the wickedness of my people Israel . . . therefore I will do to the house which is called by my name, and in which you trust, and to the place which I gave to you and to your ancestors, as I did to Shiloh. And I will cast you out of my sight, as I cast out all your kinfolk, all the offspring of Ephraim. (Jer 7:12-15; cf. 26:6)

Jerusalem is theologically like Shiloh and so is subject to the same covenant sanctions from Yahweh. Whereas the Psalm *contrasts* Jerusalem and northern alienations, the prophetic text proposes a close *parallelism*.[17] In the prophetic rendition of the tradition, the contrast between Shiloh and Jerusalem, which served Jerusalem's interests, is soundly rejected. In this Psalm, however, which is celebrative of the Jerusalem establishment, it is this contrast which is the point of the recital, whereby the Jerusalem establishment gains legitimation. The God who has utterly rejected is the God who has chosen afresh; Israel is invited by Yahweh into *a new political possibility*. Reference to the Jeremiah texts suggests that there were rival readings of the tradition, each serving a particular theological, political interest.

II

MAKING
A
WORLD

With these varied emphases on *obedience, petition, gratitude,* and *new political possibility,* the Psalms perform a variety of social functions. They are, however, agreed in their general articulation through which Israel may discern and live its life differently. In different ways, the Psalms attest to Yahweh's sovereign faithfulness and to Israel's need to come to terms with that sovereign fidelity. The Psalms invite Israel in every generation to participate in the drama of fidelity with Yahweh, a fidelity which is asserted as the most elemental and reliable fact in Israel's life. That fidelity, moreover, is sovereign. Israel must therefore receive the fidelity on terms other than its own.

Put most succinctly, these Psalms "make a world."[18] They create, evoke, suggest, and propose a network of symbols, metaphors, images, memories and hopes so that "the world," in each successive generation, is perceived, experienced, and practiced in a specific way. *The world enacted by these Psalms of recital is intergenerational, covenantally shaped, morally serious, dialogically open, and politically demanding.*

1. The world proposed in these Psalms is *inter-generational.* The very recital of the normative memory (which is known and stylized in Israel) asserts that what previous generations have done matters to the present generation, and what the present generation does is decisively shaped by choices made in times

past. The present generation both answers for and lives with the consequences of past actions. It lives from the decisions made in times past that have been remembered and transmitted.[19]

2. The world proposed in these Psalms is *covenantally shaped*. That is, there is a sovereign ruler who is bound to Israel in mutual loyalty, and that sovereign ruler cannot be ignored. Yahweh, the God of covenant-making, and Israel are together moral agents in the historical process. They must come to terms with each other. How they interact with each other matters decisively for Israel's public life and destiny. The two parties have enormous freedom and flexibility in relation to each other, but neither party is, or can ever be, completely free of the other. Each party is shaped by and destined for the other.[20] History in Israel is the on-going narrative account of that inescapable and definitional interaction.[21]

3. The world proposed in these Psalms, because of its covenantal shape, is *morally serious*. The Psalms are not simply a statement about free gifts and promises from Yahweh or glad songs by Israel. This world is powered and characterized by transactions of faithfulness and unfaithfulness, by Israel's obedience to covenantal requirements, and by Yahweh's fidelity to covenantal promises and practice of covenantal sanctions.

The action and conduct of Israel (as well as the initiatives and responses of Yahweh) may be positive or negative in relation to such a covenantal framework. Neither Israel's conduct nor Yahweh's conduct, however, can fall outside or escape serious moral, ethical assessment according to the initial terms of the relation. Israel's world consists in a powerful holy will and a responding human will, each related to the other in covenantal ways. Israel's life with Yahweh is an on-going process of yielding, resisting, submitting, asserting, and being judged and cared for by a sovereign who lives in tension with Israel's will. What Israel does not only matters to Yahweh. What Israel does goes far in determining what Yahweh will do in turn, what life Israel may live, and what future will be given to Israel by Yahweh. That Yahweh takes Israel's acts seriously means that in this "world," Israel has enormous freedom and responsibility for shaping and choosing its own destiny (cf. Jer 18:7-10). The world of these Psalms never sets aside such moral decisiveness, either for the sake of political autonomy or in the interest of religious self-indulgence.[22]

4. The world proposed in these Psalms is *dialogically open.* Each partner can do new things and neither partner is simply fated by past action.[23] At some point along the way, one might expect that the utter graciousness of Yahweh, the utter sovereignty of Yahweh, or the zealous recalcitrance of Israel might have "settled" and fated the relation (and therefore the future of Israel and of the world) for good or for ill. One might expect that Israel's life would eventually be established solely by the power of God's fidelity for security and well-being, or that Israel's life would eventually be judged simply by the rule of God for Israel's propensity to deathliness and distrust.

That kind of settlement, however, is not asserted in these Psalms. Rather, the relation is endlessly open, kept short of a final conclusion.[24] There is always the assumption and expectation that there will be a new gesture, either by Yahweh or by Israel, that will permit the world of Israel to be transformed. Even when the Psalms seem to have reached their rhetorical conclusion and their point of covenantal extremity, matters are kept open for new possibility. Thus after the long recital of sin, Psalm 106 nonetheless petitions for rescue. After the long recital of joy in Psalm 105, the concluding assertion is a summons to obedience. In both Psalms 105 and 106, the final statement moves boldly against the grain of the preceding extended argument:

> . . . to the end that they should keep God's statutes,
>   and observe God's laws. (Ps 105:45)

> Save us, O Lord our God,
>   and gather us from among the nations,
> that we may give thanks to your holy name
>   and glory in your praise. (Ps 106:47)

The recital, in both cases, is not aimed at a conclusion, but at a fresh starting point in which new decisions are made.

The world operative between Yahweh and Israel is open. It is *dialogically* open, by which I am suggesting that speech, language, and rhetoric matter enormously to the constitution of Israel's world. The vitality and restlessness of Israel's speech protest against and characteristically resist the closing of the historical process. Israel's speech will not finally accept either mute defeat or mute arrogance, because Israel and the God of Israel refuse every temptation to muteness. There is always more to be said, always one other voice to speak it, always more which Israel must hear and accept. That is why in Israel there is always one more text. In Israel one must go on speaking, either in thanks or in petition, and one must expect to be addressed and answered by Yahweh, either in promise, in command, or in verdict. Thus Israel's world is a world of peculiar and persistent dialogical speech wherein life consists of address and answer. The rhetorical resolve of Israel corresponds to the theological character of Israel's life which, like Israel's speech, is kept open and unconcluded. Israel's history does not end, because both Yahweh and Israel characteristically and relentlessly have more to say, always more to say.

It is true that Psalm 78 is less open than the other Psalms in this grouping, for it does enunciate a Davidic "settlement." Insofar as this Psalm arrives at a settlement and is unlike the other Psalms of recital, we may say that it has been skewed for ideological purposes and departs from the main tendency of Israel's narrative recital.[25] And even in this Psalm, we may notice that the Zion-David claim is not permitted a final closure. On the one hand, the critique of Jer 7:12-5 and 26:9 also belongs to this speech tradition and refuses to let the claims of Jerusalem ideology achieve a kind of settled muteness.

On the other hand, even in subsequent Davidic recitals, it is clear that the settlement cannot stay settled. One clear example of the unsettling of the Davidic settlement within the David tradition is Psalm 89. While "absolute claims" are made for David as the carrier of Yahweh's fidelity (Ps 89:19-37), the Psalm nonetheless ends with unsettling, unsettled, unanswered, pathos-filled questions (vss. 46-51). Psalm 78 is not "absolute" enough to expel Psalm 89 from Israel's life with Yahweh, and therefore from Israel's text. Nor is it powerful enough to expel from Israel's faith the awareness of historical brokenness and the hint of God's infidelity.

5. The world proposed in these Psalms is *politically demanding*. These Psalms are not mere religious statements, but they summon Israel to political discernments as a people in the world, and to political decisions about how to arrange power in the world.[26] The political freightedness of the world proposed in the Psalm of recital is especially evident in the ideological tilt of Psalm 78. The rejection of Joseph (the northern hegemony, and presumably Saul's rule; vss. 59-67) and the corresponding choice of Jerusalem (a southern hegemony and the rule of David; vss. 68-72) are of course not disinterested.[27] This example from Psalm 78 is an extreme case. It is not, however, different in kind from the claims of the other recitals.

The other Psalms of recital also hint at tilted political interests and commitments. When a recital reaches the extreme limit of Psalm 78, its proposed world can no longer stay dialogically open. The concrete political urgings of the text are too obvious and explicit, and it wants to terminate the conversation about the future. Psalm 78 gives clear expression to the tension between theological openness and concrete political commitment that is everywhere at issue for Israel.[28]

III

UNMAKING
A
WORLD

The world proposed in these Psalms is an invitation and an affirmation. It is at the same time a protest and a polemic.[29] The Psalms not only propose and constitute a world; they intend also to unmake, deconstruct, and unmask other worlds which seduce and endanger Israel, which are regarded in these recitals as false and destructive.[30] Liturgy is always and every-where world construction, and therefore necessarily *world-deconstruction* as well.

1. The world protested against in these Psalms is a *one-generational world* in which the present generation may imagine itself as uninvolved in and not impinged upon by what has already happened in Israel. The temptation to absolutize the present moment always seeks to discount the connections between generations, between past and present, and between present and future (Jer 2:5-8; cf. Ps 78:5-8).[31] An attempt to absolutize the present turns politics into an ideological project, and systematically silences both ever-present suffering and ever-dangerous hopes.

2. The world protested against in these Psalms is *devoid of authoritative covenanting*. Either in arrogance or in abdication, either by claiming everything for one's self or by turning every-thing over to God, Israel is tempted to escape from the gifts and commands that belong to covenant. Autonomy which jettisons

26

the covenant partner may be expressed as arrogance or as abandonment. In its arrogance, one may conclude, "No one sees me" (Isa 47:10) or "The Lord will not do good or ill (Zeph 1:12; cf. Jer 5:12). Expressed as abandonment, one may conclude, "My God has forgotten me" (Isa 49:14; Ps 10:11). The temptation to abdicate may be embodied in Job's friends who submit without question, who trust completely in "the rules" which they regard as "the rule of God." In any of these forms, arrogance, abandonment, or abdication, there is no costly, demanding, life-giving interaction capable of surprise. The elimination of covenanting reduces life to a flat, stable, hopeless enterprise, frozen in the happenstance of the present moment.

3. The world protested against in these Psalms is one of *moral indifference*. In that world, God is falsely discerned as having only self-indulgent concerns (cf. Ps 50:9-13; Jer 5:12; Zeph 1:12), without an intense ethical, political, economic agenda. Where God is misunderstood in this way, human life can be safely and legitimately reinterpreted and reduced to matters of money, power, cleverness, influence, security, and comfort. In place of covenant transactions, there are only commodities.[32] In such a construal, covenantal obedience, covenantal possibility, and covenantal risk disappear from public practice. When it is forgotten that God cares intensely about issues of justice and righteousness, then it quickly follows that human persons and human institutions can also scuttle such concerns. The abrogation of the commandments permits self-serving, self-indulgent forms of public life.[33]

4. The world protested against in these Psalms is one that is *monologically closed*. There is no serious life-risking, life-giving conversation, no unresolved openness that lets newness appear in the community. Such a closed world is premised on the notion that all the powerful words have already been spoken. There is nothing more left to say or to hear (Jer 7:13; 35:17; Hos 7:7; Isa 50:2). When speaking and hearing are stopped, history comes to an end.[34] Every possibility is contained in a larger, non-negotiable necessity.

5. The world protested against in these Psalms is a world of *political indifference* in which the great issues with Yahweh have been reduced to safe, religious routinization (Amos 5:21-4; 6:4-6; Isa 58:2-5). There is in such religious naivete an un-awareness of political interest, a failure to notice political ideology, a lack of courage to critique ideology. The outcome of such indifference is a failure to critique how enmeshed one inevitably is in the issues of power, legitimacy, and ideological justification. And when one is unaware, one is likely to be a helpless, unwitting instrument of those who are more cunning and more intentional.

Thus it is clear that these Psalms not only propose a world. In fact they articulate a *counter-world*, offered as a subversive alternative to the dominant, easily available worlds that are ever present in and tempting for Israel. The dominant, easily available world endlessly seducing Israel is one- generational, devoid of covenanting, morally indifferent, monologically closed, and politically indifferent. These Psalms voice a counter-world that practices exactly what the dominant world resists and denies. In its liturgic recital over a long period of time, Israel regularly enacted and embraced this counter-world as its true home.[35] Israel kept this proposed world visible, available, and legitimate by engaging in the rhetoric of recital and narrative that sustained this world. The key act in sustaining this world is to keep the memory of Israel present and powerful. It is this memory that authorizes Israel's world-creating rhetoric, and it is this articulated memory that gives Israel's world peculiar character and claim.[36] The counter-world of these Psalms (kept alive through the covenantal rhetoric of praise, thanksgiving, and petition) is a relentless, indefatigable alternative to the ever present, compelling worlds that may be technological, positivistic, morally indifferent, self-sufficient, and finally fated. Thus "history *in* Israel" is the Israelite insistence upon this rhetoric that mediates a reliable past and evokes a particular present.[37] History in Israel is a very particular linguistic practice which is a vehicle for a specific conversation about social power and social possibility.[38]

IV

ABIDING
ASTONISHMENT

Israel's historical recital is a stylized retelling of its past, and therefore an intentional shaping of the present and a passionate yearning for a specific future. Israel's maintenance of its memory through its rhetorical practice is cast in a mode which appears odd in terms of our conventional modern categories of "explanation" and "understanding." In one way, to be sure, that oddity concerns *the centrality of God* in the narrative account. The oddity is a theological oddity, on the surface an appeal to "supernaturalism." Behind that unembarrassed theological claim, however, the crucial oddity in Israel's mode of history is *the ingression of what is new*, the intrusion of something underived and unextrapolated, inexplicable in conventional terms of cause and effect. Moreover, the ingression of newness shatters all that has been, and permits the life of Israel (and of the world) to be perceived and lived in a totally new and different way. Israel's rhetorical rendering of this awesome ingression terms the inexplicable newness a "wonder" (*pela'*) and names the agent and sponsor of the wonder, the one who is newly disclosed and present in the wonder, as "God."[39]

Israel strains to find language for the ingressions of Yahweh which make all things new:

> One generation shall laud your works to another,
> and shall declare your mighty acts.
> On the glorious splendor of your majesty,
> and on your wondrous works I will meditate.

The might of your awesome deeds shall be proclaimed,
and I will declare your greatness.
They shall pour forth the fame of your abundant goodness,
and shall sing aloud of your righteousness. (Ps 145:4-7)

It is of course thinkable that terms other than "wonder" and "God" might have been used to characterize and witness to the newness. In Israel, however, these terms of rhetoric are irreplaceable and non-negotiable in the articulation of the past.

Thus "history in Israel," that is, the rendering of a powerfully present past, from now on must use the language of "wonder" and "Yahweh" as the only adequate way to speak about the newness which constitutes and generates the human, social process. The conventional language of reportage is recognized as inadequate for the power, depth, significance, density, and oddity of these remembered events around which Israel's identity and historical present are shaped. Israel can employ no other language than the language of "wonder" and "Yahweh" to transmit and testify to the new shaping of experience and memory. Transmission and testimony give coherence and identity to this community.

Martin Buber provided a most elegant comment on this peculiar characterization of history in Israel, when he discerned that Israel's history begins in miracle:

> The concept of miracle which is permissible from the historical approach can be defined at its starting point as *an abiding astonishment*. The philosophizing and the religious person both wonder at the phenomenon, but the one neutralizes his wonder in ideal knowledge, while the other abides in wonder; no knowledge, no cognition, can weaken his astonishment. Any causal explanation only deepens the wonder for him. The great turning-points in religious history are based on the fact that again and ever again an individual and a group attached to him wonder and keep on wondering; at a natural phenomenon, at a historical event, or at both together; always at something which intervenes fatefully in the life of this individual or this group. They sense

and experience it as a wonder. This, to be sure, is the only starting-point of the historical concept of wonder, but it cannot be explained away. Miracle is not something "supernatural" or "superhistorical," but an incident, an event which can be fully included in the objective, scientific nexus of nature and history; the vital meaning of which, however, for the person to whom it occurs, destroys the security of the whole nexus of knowledge for him, and explodes the fixity of the fields of experience named "Nature" and "History." Miracle is simply what happens; insofar as it meets people who are capable of receiving it, or prepared to receive it, as miracle. The extraordinary element favors this coming together, but it is not characteristic of it; the normal and ordinary can also undergo a transfiguration into miracle in the light of the suitable hour.[40]

History begins in miracle. History begins in an event of "abiding astonishment." That it is astonishing, that it provokes wonder, means that the event defies our conventional explanations and resists our intellectual domestications. There is in the event something overwhelming and overriding which does not submit to our modes of intellectual, analytical mastery. Moreover the awesomeness of the happening endures, continuing to claim and redefine the community that is beset by astonishment. Subsequent events in that community are submitted to this initial astonishment, illuminated by it, and perceived differently through it.[41] This ingression "explodes the fixity." It shatters all pre-existing categories and explanations about our discernment of both nature and history. Buber's characterization insists that this wonder is not a happening "out of the world," but belongs to the "objective, scientific nexus of nature and history." That is, the dimension of wonder must be accepted as a datum (albeit inexplicable) in the characterization and account of what happened.

Buber's analysis is made specific in his next paragraph. It is clear he speaks not of a general philosophy of history, but of a real event:

> The historical reality of Israel leaving Egypt cannot be grasped if the conception of the accompanying, preceding, guiding God is left out.[42]

The Exodus, and therefore the character of Israel, "cannot be grasped" without decisive reference to God. That is, the Exodus is sure to be misunderstood without acknowledgment of the cruciality of God. Buber continues:

> What is vital is only that what happened was experienced, while it happened, as the act of God. The people saw in whatever it was they saw "the great hand" [Ex 14:31] and they "believed in YHVH," or more correctly translated, they gave their trust to YHVH.[43]

Thus Buber rejects the liberal convention that the Bible has events which are *interpreted* as miracle.[44] The miraculous quality of Israel's past is not later attributed, but is immediately discerned as intrinsic to the act and the experience. Notice that Buber has not appealed to a supernaturalism to justify Israel's odd experience of the historical, but has in fact listened to the linguistic rendering which is required and accepted in Israel, required by the quality of the event itself. What happened in Israel is experienced and therefore must be articulated as wonder beyond any false, reductionist, "natural" explanation.

Emil Fackenheim has explored and illuminated the implications of Buber's eloquent formulation.[45] Fackenheim articulates formal, critical categories by which Buber's insight can be treated more programmatically. He suggests that in Israel's "root experiences" which generate history, three conditions are present:

a. The dialectical relation between past and present, so that the past can legislate to the present.

b. The public, historical character of events, so that they are available for public recognition and public criticism.

c. The accessibility of the past to the present, particularly the past experience of God's presence, so that subsequent generations have access to the presence of God known in the past event.[46]

32

Three factors are present in the events which serve as Israel's root experiences. They are:

a. The immediate presence of the "sole Power" in the natural-historical event.

b. The natural-historical event itself.

c. Abiding astonishment that allows the "sole Power" to be present, known, and recognized. The "sole Power" is present where the abiding astonishment is reenacted.[47]

Buber and Fackenheim do not engage in special pleading for Jewish memory, nor do they request privileged treatment for the God of Israel or for the history of Israel in our assessment of these remembered events. Rather they seek, as critically as they can, to ask what must have been present in these historical happenings that had the power and authority to generate such a dangerous, passionate historical memory. That is, they seek to take the events on their own terms in relation to the available narrated account. More than that cannot be expected of any historian.

Buber and Fackenheim make a crucial point about Israel's experience, Israel's memory, Israel's rendering of its past, and Israel's present self-understanding in light of that experienced, rendered past. None of these are second-handedly theological.[48] That is, God (or with Fackenheim, the "sole Power") is not a late addendum to the memory as a second level interpretive device. Rather God belongs integrally, inalienably, and definitionally to the event itself. Fackenheim's three factors ("sole Power," natural-historical event, and "abiding astonishment") converge in this remembered experience. "Abiding astonishment" is acknowledged as deriving from and pointing to the "sole Power" as crucial to the event. One cannot deny the "abiding astonishment," and therefore one cannot deny presence of the "sole Power" who generates the astonishment.

If one were to recast Israel's memory in order to eliminate these two factors, that is, to deny "abiding astonishment" and so expel "the sole Power," one would have left only "the natural-historical event." On the basis of the narrated account, that could not be the event that Israel experienced and remembered. Such a "natural-historical" event, stripped of its power, would not be originary or generative for Israel as the event clearly is.

The historical Psalms (with which we began our analysis) derive from and testify to this originary event and its enduring generative power. Indeed the Psalms intend to reenact the abiding astonishment of the original experience. The Psalmic recitals, which eventuate in *obedience, petition, gratitude*, and *new political possibility*, seek to do two things. First, they seek to make available to subsequent generations the experience and power of the initial astonishment which abides with compelling authority. They seek to do so even in a later time when such a "sole Power" is less available and less sought after, when such an astonishment has less credibility.[49] That is, the Psalms continue to insist on the normative power of these originary events, even in the face of a very different, more "realistic" reading of historical reality.

Second, by continuing and extending the recital beyond the originary events into monarchal history (as does Psalm 78), the recital affirms that this Yahwistic, "astonished" way of discerning Israel's present, on-going life is as valid as was the initial astonished discernment of Yahweh in the past. Thus these Psalms affirm that Israel's present (even royal, "Enlightenment") history is to be perceived in the same modes and categories of astonishment. I submit then that the on-going testimony of these Psalms in the later period is both affirmative and polemical. The recital affirms the normative quality of the "root experiences" and their categories as abidingly normative for Israel's on-going historical reality. History is indeed an arena of astonishment where the "sole Power" continues to the present. The recital polemicizes against the false attempts of *Realpolitik* to perceive and present Israel's life without reference to the "sole Power" and without the enactment and acknowledgment of abiding astonishment. That is, Israel's speech about these ingressions of God's newness necessarily concerns the claim that "God's steadfast love endures forever" (Ps 136:1ff), even into the present where *Realpolitik* appears to be decisive. The events marked as gifts of *hesed* belong to Israel's speech and Israel's claim of reality. The affirmation of *hesed* overrides every notion of *Realpolitik*.

Israel's recital is an insistence not simply on the significance of these specific events in the past, but on these odd moves of articulation as normative for discerning all events in the present and in time to come. That is, the recitals make a claim not only for normative "events," but for normative rhetoric.

In the monarchical period, when other forms of power, discernment, and accountability seems more trustworthy and more effective, it is the prophets who continue to bear witness and appeal to these categories of discernment. The prophets regularly assert the claim that the God who acted in the past acts in the same characteristic way in the present. Israel's present is to be lived and read in the same categories, they insist, as Israel's memory provides.

V

CANONICAL
RECITAL

This normative recital of Israel's past has two characteristic functions which warrant terming the recital as "canonical," as von Rad has termed it. First, this normative recital insists that these events are paradigmatic, and that all subsequent events in Israel's history are to be understood in terms of "sole Power" and "abiding astonishment,"[50] that is, as events in which the weighty, intrusive, sovereign power of Yahweh is operative and decisive. On the other hand, the canonical recital affirms with equal paradigmatic power that Israel's characteristic role in its decisive experiences is a response of trust and obedience, of glad submission, yielding either praise or repentance. That is, the Psalms yield a world which is theologically reliable and coherently ordered by the rule of Yahweh. This two-fold canonical insistence, a) that historical reality is perceived with theological *awe*, and b) that historical reality is reliably and coherently *ordered* by Yahweh, is definitional to Israel. Israel knows no other way to speak about past or present. Israel knows no other way to respond to or participate in the decisive moments in its own life.

In the following analysis, I will seek to explore two ways in which this canonical account of Israel's past is problematic, two ways that stand in stark contradiction to each other.

VI

HISTORY
AND
MODERNITY

The first problematic concerning this canonical account is the problem of a modernist perspective: modern interpreters of Israel's history find the claim of the holy, sovereign power of Yahweh as operative and decisive not only extraneous as an historical datum, but untenable.[51] It is important to recognize that modern "history of Israel" scholarship has introduced a wholly new topic with the change of the preposition from "history *in* Israel" to "history *of* Israel." The change reflects the posture of modern historiography which views Israel's history as a detached outsider without access to the astonishment which belongs intrinsically and definitionally to the recital. That is, what is confessed as normative in Israel is something other than that which is studied by our modern historiography.[52] It is remarkable that Buber and especially Fackenheim work with critical modes of analysis, and yet do so as committed "insiders." Their capacity to be insiders does not derive from their being "Jewish," as though a non-Jew must necessarily be a critical, detached outsider. The change from "insider" to "outsider," from *in* to *of*, is of a different sort. However that change is understood, the detached, modern observer is consigned to an analysis which by definition screens out and discounts the originary power of the memory.

The central assumption of the dominant contemporary historiography of ancient Israel is that the task of the historian is to "reconstruct" Israel's history, according to the best critical canon of contemporary scholarship.[53] Presentations like the historical Psalms are indeed recognized as "constructions" of Israel's history, but those materials offer "constructions" that are unacceptable, according to the requirements of modern historiography. The modern "reconstruction" is to be done by methods that are "naturalistic, empiricist, and agnostic, at best, toward claims of anything 'real' lying behind the limits of the natural (and social) orders of human experience."[54] Such an approach rejects elements that are "contaminated" and products of imagination.[55] There is a growing consensus that a viable historical reconstruction of Israel's history can only begin with David (or Solomon) and the monarchy, because only here do we have the kind of "data" which is reliable and acceptable. Prior to the emergence of the monarchy we have less "facts" than pious "fictions" of over-zealous apologists who have distorted fact with theological reference.[56] It follows, of course, that the substantive claims and rhetorical articulations of the historical Psalms are dismissed as irrelevant for "historical" presentation, and the elements of covenantal transaction that they stress and value—*obedience, petition, gratitude,* and *new political possibility*—are reckoned as illicit for historical reconstruction. That is, the reconstruction must proceed without acknowledgment of those factors which were decisive in shaping the world of ancient Israel.[57]

In this perspective on historical reconstruction about which there is a broad, rough consensus, important decisions about acceptable modes of "data" are made, almost without acknowledgment and certainly without any discomfort. These include the following.

1. *Written materials* are reliable, whereas oral materials are suspect and unreliable, if not entirely dismissable.[58] The ground for beginning the reconstruction with the monarchy is that monarchies provide materials that are official, legitimate, and orderly, and reflect great public events. This sort of testimony seems more reliable (even if it requires criticism) than the poems of barren women or grateful slaves.

2. The *evidence for states*, written and archaeological, is more enduring and more reliable than the flimsy rhetorical efforts of pre-state tribal and clan groupings. States have the power to construct reality in formal ways and with adequate claims of legitimacy to make the construction "real" and "enduring." The state with its ordered power lives in a "real" world of power and control, in a way that the cries and yearnings of the disordered, powerless wretched do not.[59] It is ironic that the claims of the state endure through monuments and official documents, whereas in the pre-state statements, all that abides is "astonishment." Such a bias toward "state truth" seems to accept too readily the power of the state to reconstruct the past to serve its own ends.[60] This bias toward state truth is a common one for established historians. That same propensity is present in Old Testament historiography which focuses on the "record" of the state.

3. The *evidence of "facts"* is so much more reliable than appeal to "miracles," for miracles smack of other-worldliness, naivete, romanticism, and unreality.[61] The terms "fact" and "miracle" rest uneasily in the same conversation. The two terms in practical usage reflect different social locations and political interests. Preference for "fact" is a claim characteristically made by those with power to legitimate their own reading of reality; "miracle" most often comes to us on the attestation of those who lack social power to legitimate in conventional ways their claims, and who engage in hope and imagination which are incongruous with the realities of established power. That is, "fact" and "miracle" do not concern simply *modes of knowledge* but also the legitimating claims and assumptions that authorize alternative *modes of power*. The attraction of "fact" in our modern reconstructions of the past seems to tilt the historical process toward established power rather than wonder, so that the reliable material for history is material that is allied with established power.

4. The modern inclination is to study *patterns of control* to the exclusion of inexplicable gifts. That is, control is the extreme form of human initiative, and history is a reconstruction of the

lines of power and authority, a tale of initiatives taken, wars won and lost, based on emblems of control such as walls, monuments, and inscriptions.[62] Systematically excluded from such a field of data are gifts given which stress human receptivity and not human initiative, receptivity which leaves no later traces of power, but only traces of rhetoric bespeaking obedience, petition, gratitude, and new political possibility, all embraces of wonder.

5. The modern inclination is to weave an historical account of *cause and effect*, to see what gave rise to what.[63] An account is constructed which eliminates slippage (mystery), which discounts any inexplicable *novum*, which explains away any staggering act *ex nihilo* that may originate and live outside human choice, human control, human initiative, and human will.

My point is not to resist the dismissal of "the supernatural," a dismissal which is standard in modern reconstructions of Israel's history. It is rather to notice the bias, interest, and predictable outcome of these choices made by modern historians in the reconstruction of Israel's past. Modern, critical reconstructions are based on a series of choices which value a) *writing*, b) *state-story*, c) *fact*, d) *control*, and e) *cause and effect*, and conversely, which disregard an alternatives of a) *oral testimony*, b) *clan-story*, c) *miracle*, d) *gift*, and e) *slippage*. I offer these lists as suggestive and impressionistic, for the categories need to be much refined. These contrasts are, however, sufficient to make the point that "objective" historical reconstructions reflect powerful ideological commitments.

The issue I wish to raise is not based on a "theological protectionism" which is unhappy with "the expulsion of God" from the historical process.[64] The issue rather concerns the long-term implication of such "naturalistic, empirical, and agnostic" scholarship. Henry Kissinger has opined in an unguarded but characteristic statement that "history consists in what states do."[65] In a more anecdotal form, Ronald Reagan has polemically insisted that "news" is what happens at the center of power.[66] One would not of course wish to identify too closely the cynicism of Kissinger or the insensitivity of Reagan with scholars who pursue the objectivist modes of historical reconstruction noted above. Nonetheless, these verdicts of Kissinger and Reagan and much contemporary critical practice come very close to the same result. The effort to avoid supernaturalism, to guard against history as code language for theological confession, and to reject "theological protectionism," has reduced historical reconstruction to the affairs of state and to the initiatives, control, and legitimacy of powerful persons and powerful institutions.

History then has to do primarily with "affairs of state"— territory, war, succession, and temples which are allied with the self-serving "reasons of state." In such a portrayal of Israel's past, what drops out of consideration are the laments of bereaved women, the protests of raging prophets, the cries of the poor, and the promises of the poets, because laments, protests, cries, and promises are not the stuff of "history," but only the imagination and religious "contamination" of the marginal. What is dismissed in such an account is not only the reality of God, crucial as that is in these recitals, but the reality of human hurt and human hope, the stricken bodies of those who hurt, and the tensive alternatives of those who hope. Modernist historiography imagines it can reconstruct the past without reference to the rhetoric and generative power of hurt and hope.[67]

Scholars who sort things out in our now conventional, "scientific" way are guided (as we currently are in the academy), by "objectivity," an objectivity that does not consort with confession or with theological "ideology."[68] The mode of objectivity thus embraced is the practice of "autonomous reason," reason that grants no privilege or priority to special religious pleading, pleading which is now pejoratively identified, in the language of social science, as "ideology."[69]

The problem with this kind of "objectivity" and its autonomous reason is that, in the end, "the autonomy of reason" is linked to "the autonomy of power." Power practiced in the ancient world thus reconstructed, is not contextualized, authorized, or assessed by any moral framework. Reduced to simpler

41

formulation, when history is the action of the state (Solomonic or otherwise), we are left with the judgment that "might makes right." The elimination of obedience, petition, gratitude, and fresh political possibility as mere rhetoric which contaminates factuality leaves no basis from which to make human assessments of what happened in the ancient world.

My purpose is not to criticize any particular reconstruction of Israel's history, nor to deny the problematic character of the available data, but to raise for consideration the question of cost and implications of our current commitment to the "objective" "reconstruction" of Israel's history.[70] The embrace of "objectivity" and the purging of "supernaturalism" lead, I suggest, to history "from above," a reconstruction preoccupied with the public management of power. It is ironic if the primary tendency of such an "objective" enterprise is to make modernist reconstructions an ally of ancient tyranny, if the modern "autonomy of reason" is an unwitting legitimator of an ancient "autonomy of power."[71]

It is worth considering a "sociology of wonder," and asking who is open to "abiding astonishment," and who might be compelled to overcome, banish, or deny such astonishment? I submit that "abiding astonishment," the celebration of enduring miracle, tends not to occur among those who manage writing, who control the state, who create and transmit proper "facts," who monopolize control, and who explain by cause and effect. The experience and articulation of "wonder" tends to occur in the midst of oral expression, in simpler social units, among those who yearn for and receive miracle, who live by gift since they have little else by which to live, and who are sustained only by slippage (mystery) and gaps in the dominant system of power. The elimination of "wonder" from historical reconstruction thus is a drastic decision to read historical memory in the presence and service of one sociological interest, at the great expense of a contrasting social interest.[72]

I propose that the old question left by von Rad concerning the relation of "secular history" and "salvation history" may need to be reexamined and reformulated. Could it be that what we call "secular history" is in fact history "from above," preempted by those in power who require and permit no historical act or explanation beyond their own control, and who are willing to take whatever initiatives that need to be taken for the maintenance of their own power?[73] Conversely, "salvation history" may be the desperate rhetoric of the powerless and marginal who have no access to public, formal power. They must therefore rely on the thickness of their rhetoric, and the energy, courage, freedom, and gift generated by that rhetoric, whereby transformation may be wrought, and new miracles generated, out of old memories of astonishment.[74]

Thus the preference for "secular history" over "salvation history" may be based on a disregard for the relative social location of the two perspectives and for their respective deployments of language as power. The easy preference for "secular history" betrays an insensitivity to the force of language and the connection between social power and linguistic construal of reality. It also may fail to acknowledge that certain rhetorical construals of the past may be the only social power of those who by any other social norm are utterly without power.

Our conventional assumption (given the course of modern, intellectual development) is that "scientific history" supersedes "salvation history" as we become more urbane, more rational, and more intellectually self-aware. Such an evolutionary scheme regards the "earlier" modes of historical rhetoric as primitive, naive, and unsophisticated, surely not legitimate material for our "objective reconstruction."[75] If, however, "secular history" and the autonomy of reason are allied with concentrations of force and the autonomy of power, then perhaps "salvation history" is not primitive and not to be superseded by more sophisticated epistemology, but is in fact counter-history, a recital to challenge "from below" the great, established account of social reality.[76] "Salvation history" then is a revision of memory that brings to speech those silenced in powerlessness and marginality. Such counter-history may be the determined insistence that the long silenced voice of hurt and hope cannot be finally silenced by the facts of brutish or rationalized power.

The historical Psalms, with their hoped for outcomes of obedience, petition, gratitude, and fresh political possibility are not simply "primitive" and "naive"; they are, rather, determined challenges to the autonomy of reason and the autonomy of power. The Psalms relentlessly insist that power is not autonomous, but is and must be in a context of moral reality. Again, Psalm 78 poses an important exception to these claims. The critical treatment of the Psalm in the tradition of Jeremiah, however, makes clear that even the ideological claim of Psalm 78 is drawn into Israel's world of moral reality. And even in Psalm 78 itself, it is the God who is earlier vexed and gracious who does the choosing of Zion and David. These Psalms of historical recital characteristically assert that reason is not autonomous and that knowing is allied with remembering, praising, trusting, confessing, and petitioning.[77] This alternative rhetoric commends an alternative perspective on power as well as on knowledge.[78]

I suggest that "objective" "reconstructions" of Israelite history (that dismiss these Psalmic recitals as pious "imaginations" that "contaminate" fact) may function as an uncriticized ideology that is unwittingly allied with established interests, both ancient and contemporary. It may be possible to invert Long's formula in which he contrasts "theological protectionism" and "social analysis."[79] Viewed from the underside, we may suggest a "social scientific protectionism" in the name of "objectivity" which seeks to preserve an autonomous rationality, a protectionism which is challenged by a theological analysis attentive to hurt and hope. Thus I suggest that what we term "protectionism" and what we label "analysis" may indeed depend on the intellectual, epistemological, and political- economic commitments to which we knowingly or unknowingly subscribe. The labels themselves may indeed be pejorative, ideological gestures that purport to be "objective" but in effect legitimate power from above.

The "protectionism" of so-called "objectivity" (which tends to refuse to credit historical memory prior to the state) may protect the ancient historical enterprise of royal power (and by implication our own historical enterprise of domination). Such usage may protect concentrated power from a theological openness and criticism. This criticism of the "protectionism" of "objectivity" suggests that the important "real material" of history may not be found in the state which writes, and in large centers of power, but in the smaller social units that leave only oral monuments of hurt and hope. This sort of historical residue (the oral monument which occasionally becomes text) may provide the material for our historical "reconstruction." It has its predictable habitat in all the "South Succotashes" of the unemployed and marginal where the news is not of power, but of grief and hunger and yearning and possibility. Power, in this view, is not so autonomous as to be cut off from moral concerns. And knowledge is not so cut off from hurt and hope as we might wish. In these "underneath" communities, I submit, it is the rhetoric of obedience, petition, gratitude, and fresh political possibility that protests against the autonomy of reason and the autonomy of power which wants to establish itself as "objective."

I am given pause when I think of contemporary accounts of "official history" which may be analogous to our "objective accounts" of ancient Israel. Would such an analogy imply that the history of South Africa begins only with the Apartheid government of 1948? Or that the history of Nicaragua begins only with the Spanish conquistadors? Or that academic history in the United States begins and ends with male hegemony? The question in the ancient world (and in our own world) is of course not only when did history begin, but what constitutes history after it has begun? If history in South Africa may only begin in 1948, what now of the pathos-filled poems and enraged novels that trace a different past? If the history of Nicaragua is only the account of European and U.S. colonialism, what of the pain and passion of the base communities that generate another social reality? Or what of the counter-claims made in our academic communities by those who as yet control no committees or journals and are scarcely respectable?[80]

I am not sure what these questions mean for the historical reconstruction of ancient Israel. I suspect we are warned that we must not be so sure of our "objectivity," or so dismissive of "counter-rhetoric" which sounds "theological" and "ideological." Perhaps the "naivete" in Israel's historical memory is not solely where we thought it was. Perhaps while we thought these ancient songs and stories were naive, it turns out that our own passion for "objectivity" is both naive and gullible.

In the end, the Psalms of historical recital are perhaps a revision of and protest against "state accounts" of the past. That Psalmic revisionism provides a rhetoric through which to inquire about a revision of our "objective" notions of autonomous reason and autonomous power. The elimination of "abiding astonishment" from our horizons of historical reconstruction makes concentrated, legitimated power the final arbiter of the historical process. The banishment of *awe* (so passionately affirmed in these recitals) may be not only the "expulsion of God," but the forfeiture of human possibility and the nullification of serious social criticism. Our "objectivity" may be an act which grants continuous legitimacy to what was so stridently legitimated in the ancient world by the power of the dominant establishment. Our scholarly, modernist categories may be not only against "abiding astonishment," but in favor of the established force of entrenched power. Thus our modernist categories are frequently allied with states that can guarantee order.

VII

MONOPOLY
AND
MARGINALITY

The second problematic concerning this canonical recital moves in a very different direction. Interpretations grounded in modernity find the recital making appeal to "supernatural agency," an appeal which must on this view be eliminated from any serious understanding of history. (This is the point argued above.) The second problem I shall address is not a reluctance about the "supernatural agency" in these recitals, but a hard insistence on the monopoly of perspective claimed by those who are on the "inside" of the recital.[81]

Interpretation by complacent insiders who accept the rhetoric of the recitals tends to use the recital as a preferred reading of history which supports and sustains certain kinds of human domination. Functionally, then, the Psalms no longer tell of surprising rescue and well-being; now God has become entirely predictable and contained within the limits of the routinized recital. That is, the Psalms purport to give an exhausting account of what is possible from God. The practical outcome of such a controlled, stylized recital is that the sponsors and advocates of the recital have the capacity to define social reality and the social position of other members of the community.

These Psalms claim to give a full account of everything that happened in Israel that is important for memory. Surely the Psalms list all of Israel's "canonical" "root experiences." They present Israel's full account of its past as morally coherent, rendered in these Psalms in terms of God's goodness and Israel's fidelity and/or guilt. That is, the world of Yahweh's governance makes coherent sense. The Psalms reflect the experience and conviction of those who trust and know the world of Yahwistic governance to be "sense-making." The Psalms voice the faith of those who have benefitted from the wonders (and are grateful), or who have experienced the judgment of God as acceptable and credible (and so repent).[82]

Filled as it is with awe, the canonical recital in these Psalms is nonetheless an "establishment account" in ancient Israel, in which the hard issues of theodicy are denied, disregarded, or unrecognized.[83] In making this argument, I am considering an issue which is the very opposite of the point just made in Part VI. There, I argued that the Psalms are a *counter-recital* against established power which appears to be "objective." Here I argue that the recital of the Psalms is an *establishment recital* from which some are excluded who have not experienced the gifts affirmed, and who do not find the assumed system of rewards and punishments to be credible. There are those who have experienced life in shabby, painful ways which are not congruent with this recital. There are those who suffer, but who do not repent, because they know of no guilt commensurate with the repentance required by the established system of rewards and punishments.

Thus the Psalm may perform either an *imperial function* of asserting a well-ordered status quo, or a *subversive function* of undermining a well-ordered status quo. In the end, the particular rhetorical, political function of a Psalm, subversive or imperial, depends on our "theatre of interpretation." Goldingay has seen that a Psalm may be either settling or subversive, depending on use, context, and intent.[84] This general argument about the Psalms applies as well to the Psalms of historical recital. Their social, interpretive force depends on whether they are set in the midst of modernity (where they are *subversive*) or in the midst of marginality (where they are *imperial*).

The recital of the Psalms make two foundational theological claims. On the one hand, God is good, gives gifts, and rescues in response to need. On the other, the ones who suffer must repent and they will be healed. The two affirmations together propose a world of moral symmetry which is canonical and non-negotiable. Those who do not share this moral symmetry are not given voice in these Psalms.

Important elements of the experience of the Israelite community are excluded from this canon, just as the modern scientific reconstruction of the history of ancient Israel excludes some experiences. This establishment recital has no room in it for those who do not share in this persuasive and adequate drama of guilt and grace (just as the scientific account has no place in it for those who do not share in its story of power). In our own time, we are recovering the "forgotten histories" and "hidden histories" which have been excluded from our "official accounts."[85] In a parallel way, the total literature of the Bible, with its strange, undisciplined inclusiveness, preserves the voices of the voiceless whose life and faith are not in the horizon of the canonical narrative recitals.[86] It is remarkable that the sacred writings of Israel did not permit the powerful, establishment claims to drown out other voices which continue to be present, albeit marginally. The scholarship and interpretive inclination of the so-called "Biblical Theology Movement" tended to give the establishment recital such weight that other voices were largely unnoticed. Such interpretive inclinations, however, did not force those other voices out of the literature of the Bible.[87]

Consequently those voices are still present in the larger literature, still operative in the memory, and are now being heard among us in fresh ways.[88] In the face of the establishment claim that God is good, gives gifts, and rescues in response to voiced need, there are those in Israel's memory and remembered rhetoric who do not share in that affirmation, who know nothing of God's goodness, nothing of God's gifts, nothing of God's rescue, and nothing of which to repent.

First, there were those who did not experience *God's goodness*, who had experienced nothing which left "abiding astonishment," who must have sat mute and unresponsive while the Psalms were recited. The Psalms of recital (especially Psalm 136) offer an inventory of God's goodness, voiced without any qualifications. Trible and many others have given particular and sustained attention to "Texts of Terror," narrative accounts of women who are portrayed as marginal and abused in Israel's life, and whose narratives are surely at the margin of Israel's awareness *vis à vis* the normative recital.[89] These narratives are by and for those who are abused and maltreated, who either had no heart for prayer of an establishment kind, or whose prayers, when uttered, were left unnoticed and unanswered. These stories of Hagar, Tamar, and Jephthah's daughter are cited here not as evidence that the normative recital is false, but that the normative recital is not the whole story of Israel's faith and life. We do not have a text in Israel which recites in normative, stylized fashion this counter-experience, an experience of God's indifference and society's brutality. Nevertheless, it is important that in the memory and writings of Israel, those texts and experiences have not been lost or censored entirely.[90] They continue to arise "from below," forcing their ways into the normative world and into the canonical recital, declaring that the legitimated recital is partly false because it is partial.[91]

Second, there were those in Israel who no longer found *the theological grid of "guilt-punishment-repentance-forgiveness"* credible. That grid of "guilt and grace" remains credible and valid for those who in fact suffer for guilt and are forgiven. That grid is especially evident in Psalms 78 and 106. That set of theological assumptions, however, is not valid in the face of innocent sufferers who can acknowledge no serious guilt and who find nothing of which to repent.[92] In their candor and impatience, such persons conclude that their suffering and alienation from God are not due to their failure, but to a failure on God's part. For them, the important theological issue becomes God's unfaithfulness and injustice. This motif, however, does not qualify to be included in Israel's "canonical" recitals. The texts, like the experiences, inevitably remain, so to speak, "non- canonical."

This theological verdict in Israel, rooted in painful experience, evokes poems of disjunction and hostility that we place under the rubric of "theodicy."[93] The canonical recital affirms a workable, coherent "theodic settlement" in which the rewards and punishments of God are known, trusted, and accepted.[94]

Israel's "theodic crisis" arises when the sufferings no longer relate credibly to identifiable guilt. The challenge to the theological consensus of Israel's canon may be expressed as the relentless demand of Job or the exhausted resignation of Ecclesiastes.[95] Neither the silence of God (Job) nor the indifference of God (Ecclesiastes) is voiced in the establishment recital. It is nonetheless known and expressed elsewhere in Israel, outside the normative recital.

Third, the canon confesses and celebrates *Yahweh's attentive presence* to Israel, sometimes attentive as giver of gifts, sometimes attentive as moral guarantor.[96] The recital of saving deeds in Psalm 105 and the inventory of deeds of *hesed* in Psalm 136 attest to God's attentive presence as giver of gifts. Conversely Psalms 78 and 106 show God's attentiveness as moral guarantor. In the life of Israel, however, Yahweh is not always present. The laments/complaints of Israel are a counter-voice, counter to the credo. They assert Yahweh's absence, silence, eclipse, and indifference, in which there are no marvels from God at which to wonder. It is now agreed that the notion of "God's mighty deeds in history" is no adequate way to understand Israel's life or faith. It may be, however, that our recent rejection of such a notion has been for the wrong reasons, for reasons of modernity. Our intellectual framework has led us to regard the notion of "God acts in history" as intellectually untenable.

That conclusion, however, may suggest that "modernity" is not simply a situation coming after intellectual "primitivism," but that it reflects a socio-economic-epistemological situation of those who engage in autonomous reason in defense of autonomous power. That is, the rhetoric of "God's mighty deeds" is not congenial to our scientific, objectivist, positivistic control of life.[97] The ground from which we reject the notion of "God's mighty deeds" is important to identify. It must be faced, because in our contemporary world there are many people for whom the rhetoric of "abiding astonishment" is indeed credible, and for whom the "acts of God" are not failed rhetoric. The viability of such language is evident among the marginal who are hospitalized, and among the economically marginal who

51

find courage and hope in this rhetoric which yields both patience to wait and impatience for action.[98] Thus our dismissal of the language of the canonical recital on intellectual grounds is indeed tied to our economic, political situation of power.

In the dissent of those who do not experience good, who do not concede guilt, and who do not discern presence, the critique of the normative recital of God's mighty deeds is rooted in concrete historical experience which the dominant ideology cannot deny or dismiss. The problematic of Job's rage, Ecclesiastes' resignation, and Psalm 88's isolation (for example) are not intellectual rejections of normative rhetoric based on the conclusion that God does not act. Rather these responses are based on the conviction that God does indeed characteristically act, but has not acted in this case. That is, these dissents make sense, intellectually and rhetorically, only when the premise of the credo holds. It is the expectation of "abiding astonishment" that leads to the awareness and expression of painful, unbearable absence. While we, in our characteristic intellectual rejection, no longer expect to be astonished, these poignant voices of protest and lament still remember, anticipate, and insist upon such astonishment, and dread its absence.

The establishment recital and the dissents which counter that recital are intensely and dialectically related to each other. In the ancient shaping of the Bible, the literature of dissent was permitted and retained alongside the establishment recital. In the scholarship of the last two generations, under the influence of von Rad, the canonical recital was presented with such singular focus that the dissent received almost no attention.[99] In current scholarship, both influenced by modernity and in reaction against modernity, it is significant that a primary challenge to Israel's credo recital of its past is not located in Psalmic and narrative dissents of pain and indignation, but in the wisdom tradition which offers an alternative to the normative rhetoric.[100] Current attention to wisdom literature and its rhetoric concerns theological claims that are hidden and not direct, arising out of experience rather than imposed from external authority, and concerned with social order (Proverbs) and social hurt (Job), rather than the more familiar categories of guilt and rescue.

In our "objectivist" modernity, we may prefer to escape the rhetoric of the recital which manifestly is not "objective." We will, however, be closer to the world of the text itself, and closer to our own historical circumstance, if we see that the most crucial challenge to the establishment recital arises not from its "primitive" language (as with the urbaneness of wisdom), but from the dissent of pain, indignation, brutality, and resignation which issues in a counter-recital which has not yet qualified as sacred text. In the troubled places where the hurting ones find the establishment recital unconvincing (such places as Palestine, South Africa, and Latin America, and the hopeless poverty-class of our own society), the hurting ones do not reject the language of the recital, but shrilly insist on its implementation.

Among the marginal, resistance to the claims of established ideology (which usually claims a religious grounding) is not expressed as rejection of religious claims. Rather resistance is characteristically voiced as an urgent, passionate insistence that God's intention for justice and freedom should be enacted. The hurting ones count heavily upon the language of the recital, but insist that the recital must be opened for new acts of rescue and transformation. Those hurting ones have not ceased to insist on or to hope for abiding astonishment. It is telling that in our own socio-religious context, it is not the ones marginalized by the dominant power who reject its rhetoric, but the ones who escape its claims into autonomy that find such language offensive and unconvincing.[101]

There are thus two very different crises about the narrative recital. On the one hand, there is the crisis of those who reject the rhetoric of recital for the sake of autonomous reason and autonomous power. This is the crisis for those "above," those who seek to reconstruct Israel's past according to the categories of autonomy and objectivity. For them, the language of the recital must be abandoned. On the other hand, there is the crisis of those who continue to insist on the reality of the rhetoric and await its actualization. This is the crisis of those "below." For them, the rhetoric of the recital must be opened to include the counter-experience of marginalization, disregard, and brutalization.

VIII

ISRAEL'S
HISTORY

There are two quite distinct intellectual crises at work in response to the establishment recital reflected in these Psalms. The crisis "from above" is tempted to jettison Israel's canonical rhetoric in its "objective" reconstruction, and thus escape the claim of the recital by disallowing the compelling reality of astonishment. Satisfying as that strategy may be for some, it does not at all serve those in the other crisis, "from below." Those latter will not jettison the rhetoric of the normative recital, for that rhetoric is the most effective and available way to keep the justice questions alive, concerning God's goodness, equity, and presence. The autonomy so valued in our modernity may turn out to be a profound disservice to the marginalized. "Naturalist, empiricist and agnostic" reconstructions of Israel's past serve the interest of the state (or the religious establishment, or the academic establishment) against the marginalized. The marginal have no interest, as do the "tenured," in naturalist, empiricist, and agnostic reconstructions, but want instead the restoration of "conflict, ambiguity, and tragedy" into theological-political language. It is, however, precisely "conflict, ambiguity, and tragedy" which autonomous power cannot tolerate. In our reconstructions of that past, we may need to ask not only "what happened?," but what kind of language is indispensable for the maintenance of our common humanness?[102] A historical reconstruction which denies and kills the rhetoric of obedience, petition, gratitude, and fresh political possibility can hardly be true to the memory of this people, past or present, even if it is respectable to the academic world of objectivity and the established world of rationalized power.

The problem of Israel's history and its reconstruction is acute, given our Enlightenment modes of rationality and knowledge. My comments are not an urging that we should uncritically reiterate Israel's normative recital as though there were no more to be said about Israel's history. The juxtaposition of these two critical responses to the historical recital, one from positivistic historicism (the inclination of modernity which eliminates awe [holiness]), one from the sociology of marginality (which insists on justice), suggests that our now conventional reconstructions of the history of ancient Israel which focus on royal history[103] have not fully faced the problem of Israel's history, the power of its rhetoric, or the socio-political intent of its self-understanding and self-presentation.[104]

The modernist reconstruction which focuses on "what happened" tends to be insensitive to the subversive intentionality of the recital which uses the rhetoric of "abiding astonishment" to keep royal-establishment claims from being absolutized.[105] That is, the rhetoric asserting that "God acted" is not simply a naive transcendentalism or supernaturalism, but is a religio-political claim that likely cannot be expressed in any other way.[106] When contemporary reconstructions of Israel's history seek to eliminate the rhetoric of the recital, they do away with the destabilizing, subversive, and therefore hopeful dimension of Israel's historical discernment. That is, the "neutral" rendering of Israel's past silences what is definitional and crucial for discerning "what happened." What happened is that ingressive power has been released that will not be administered. To this ingress of power, Israel's memory testifies.

Conversely, the polemical posture of the marginal finds the establishment recital of the Psalms to be excessively transcendental, not in detached religious claims but in an ideological act which denies, limits, and excludes elements of the memory, so that the recital serves to assert a kind of legitimacy for the powerful who formulate the creed and who are themselves its "end result."[107] The marginal, I submit, find the creed objectionably transcendental, not because it is theological, but because its theology has such a clear, unambiguous social function of tolerating pain as acceptable social act, censoring dissent, and denying enduring injustice.[108]

Thus, on the one hand, the modernist reconstruction wants to eliminate the threat of *awe* which it finds unmanageable. The critique of the marginal, on the other hand, wants to overcome the excessive claim of *order* that is articulated in the recital at the expense of the justice questions. The elimination of the *threat of awe* is explicitly designed to permit autonomous reason to operate, and inadvertently celebrates autonomous power. The *claim of excessive order* wants to eliminate the shrillness of rage, the authority of pain, and the possibility of destabilizing hope. It is clear that a modernist critique and the critique of marginality go in opposite directions. The modernist critique of Israel's normative recital wants to eliminate the recital as a counter-construction of history with its insistence on awe, which is intellectually unmanageable. The critique of marginality wants to overcome a presentation of history which it has found excessively monopolistic in its insistence on order at the expense of justice.

I suggest that the problematic of historical reconstruction of Israel's history reflects two unreconciled dimensions of the Enlightenment.[109] The modernist effort, *derived from Kant*, is committed to the autonomy of reason, but is uncritical about how the autonomy of reason ends in the uncriticized autonomy of power. The effort of the marginal, *derived from Marx*, is committed to the legitimacy of pain, and the critique of social systems and ideologies which generate pain and legitimate it as an acceptable social reality. The unresolved interrelation of the perspectives of Kant and Marx, reflected in the modernist-marginalist criticisms of Israel's historical recital, concern the vexed question whether Israel's history shall be discerned and assessed "from above" or "from below."

What matters is what historical reconstruction is willing to let count in the reconstruction. I suggest for our future work in reconstruction, three general considerations.

1. Modes of reconstruction derived from Kant, which are taken to be objective, must take more seriously the Marxian recognition that there is no social neutrality in reconstruction. What passes for neutrality is predictably allied with the status quo, or in Israel, a partisan support for royal versions of history. Positivists must give attention both to the cost of their partisanship and to their own vested interest in such a reading.

2. Enlightenment rationality is committed to the elimination of rhetoric in the interest of facts. We can, it is assumed, have purely "factual history" when all passions of rhetoric have been silenced. The recognition that historians "reconstruct," however, means that rhetoric can never be eliminated and that history is essentially an act of rhetoric. Thus we face the simple and crucial question, what kind of rhetoric most faithfully renders the past of this community? No case has been made, known to me, that the royal annals are more reliable rhetoric than the poem, that the chronicle carries more "fact" than the lament. To be sure, the modes of rhetoric are different, but not therefore necessarily superior. Annals and chronicle do indeed reflect more stable power and more legitimated authority, but for all of that, no less vested interest.

If the historian is concerned in the work of reconstruction with "what happened," then the next question is, "*Who* should be asked?" Or, "What happened according to *whose vision*? Or, "What happened *to whom*?" That is, "what happened" depends on who speaks. Let us take a case in point. The narrative accounts of Ex 16:13 and Num 11:31 are reiterated in the canonical recital of Ps 105:40:

They asked, and God brought quails,
　　and gave bread from heaven in abundance.

Israel's classic rhetoric of the memory of quail-giving is cast in theological language of petition and response: "They asked-- God brought." This account of the memory affirms that the "event" concerned daring, insistent petition which moved Yahweh to exercise sovereign power over creation for the well-being of this people. The two crucial elements in this statement of what happened are daring speech addressed to the

57

"sole Power," and a responding generosity on the part of the "sole Power." To be sure, this is a partisan rendering of the past according to a particular pattern of rhetoric.

Consider, by contrast, what happens when this same "event" is rendered in positivistic language, "uncontaminated" by theological rhetoric. Wright says of this same event:

> After crossing the sea, they [quails] land on the Sinai shore, completely exhausted and are easily caught.[110]

Clearly something is gained in Wright's rendering, for now the "event" is "explained." Notice that even Wright's rendering is a rendering, that is, a choice of a certain rhetoric. It could not be otherwise. The "event" now, in the language of Wright, is controllable and understandable according to scientific categories from which an embarrassing theological claim has been removed.[111] What is lost in Wright's rendering is the cruciality of petition, the awe of response, and the astonishment of gift. Wright's explanatory rhetoric has expelled from Israel's memory the asking and answering, and the gift. The memory has been robbed of any abiding astonishment. The "event" has been explained in such a way that it has no future.[112]

The historian has asked, "what happened?" When the answer is given, it is an answer unavoidably given in some mode of speech, which is always partisan, never objective. A modern scholar (such as Wright) may indeed tell us "what happened." When a singer in Israel, however, tells us "what happened," it is a different telling. That singer would not imagine or concede that what happened was quail falling, "completely exhausted." What happened was a very different event, freighted with wonder, evoked by speech, requiring gratitude and awe, celebrating an ingress of newness. Such a singer could never be talked out of this rendering, nor persuaded of a modernist rendering.[113]

3. Historical reconstruction must ask, "What is the on-going character of this people and this text as they continue to be present in the contemporary world?" Since we are agreed that the historical task is one of "reconstruction," inquiring about the contemporary presence of people and book is legitimate,

because every reconstruction is a present reconstruction, done now in present circumstance, with present states of knowledge and methods of interpretation. There is, in reconstruction, no simple, innocent escape possible from the present tense of reconstruction into an uncontaminated pre-rhetorical past. The historian who engages in reconstruction might wish for such protection from complicity in the present, but it is not possible. The historian lives inevitably in an intellectual world where it is no longer possible to be innocent about hermeneutics. The historian lives inevitably in a sociological world where it is no longer possible to be innocent about competing, rival readings. The historian lives inevitably in a political world of power and terrorism, of order and rage, of reenforced policing and daring dissent. The historian lives inevitably in a rhetorical world of statistical serenity and unambiguous memos, of grieving poems and subversive songs. In the presence of such intellectual awareness, sociological dispute, political conflict, and rhetorical tension, reconstruction takes place. The claim to be doing uninhibited "social analysis," as Long has suggested, is surely not viable. It is of course possible to do historical reconstruction which disregards, or pretends to disregard, the present. Such disregard, however, turns out not to be neutral, but "objectivist" in its support of established power.

What must give us pause in our reconstructive activity is that there are significant communities of memory in our world that continue to find "abiding astonishment" in these texts, astonishment that is translated into political energy and courage. These communities continue to find the rhetoric of obedience, petition, gratitude, and fresh political possibility credible language for receiving life, past and present, in the face of power, stability, and even brutality. I do not suggest that such renderings and reconstructions should be decisive for us in the academy. I urge only that they cannot be ignored by us, for to ignore them is to disregard the peculiar, subversive history enacted in ancient Israel, a subversive history that has enduring power and danger, a subversive history that can only be rendered and reconstructed in rhetoric that would never be mistaken for objectivity.[114]

In addition to the daring argument of Fackenheim, we may notice two other recent perspectives on this people, these texts, this rhetoric, this history, which pertain to our argument. First, Michael Walzer has observed that Israel's experience of the Exodus has been a memory that has continued to generate social power and social revolution.[115] Clearly the generative power of the memory has been mediated through its own raw rhetoric and not through a rendering that is "naturalistic, empiricist, and agnostic."

Second, Herbert Schnaidau has concluded that Israel's history has been an arena of historical experience oddly focused on attentiveness to the "underdog."[116] While that concern for the underdog has now become commonplace, Schnaidau urges that such a perception of historical reality was not present prior to the dangerous memory of Israel. A history in which *revolution is generated* (Walzer) and in which underdogs are prized (Schnaidau) requires a distinct rhetoric that is not neutral and analytical, a rhetoric that is bold, subversive, partisan, and passionate. It is that rhetoric which offers a sustained protest against an order which has unwittingly become brutal. It is that rhetoric which keeps open the hope for an alternative possibility. The indispensable human work of protest and possibility lives in and through this rhetoric.

It is of course possible to reconstruct the history of Israel so that it is devoid of such dimensions of revolutionary, subversive substance. Then, however, we may wonder what it is that is reconstructed. Israel's past may then be a story suitable to our "naturalistic, empiricist, and agnostic" methods and perspectives, a story which now itself is "naturalistic, empiricist, and agnostic." But what is the point of such a reconstruction? Is it a reconstruction congenial to and perhaps in the service of the established academy in which intellect has become allied with established power? Such an enterprise, I submit, is an intellectual effort unwittingly in the service of political stability, for a world without "abiding astonishment" can indeed be administered, predicted, and controlled. Such a reconstruction, I imagine, is both a betrayal of those in our present time who are not alienated by the rhetoric of Israel's memory, who live from that rhetoric, and a betrayal of those in the past who risked to generate such rhetoric and shape such texts, because that was the only way in which they could testify to what had happened.

I may of course have confused rhetoric with fact, literary analysis with historiography, theology with social analysis. Those confusions (if that is what they are) seem to me not as costly or portentous as the confusion of political alliance with scientific neutrality, which provides legitimacy for a certain kind of power in the name of objectivity. There is no simple way out of our dilemma. Our best resolve, perhaps, is that our historical reconstruction should pay heed to the very different reading of this past being conducted among the marginal. Of course that is a troublesome thought for us, for *modernity* intends precisely to screen out *marginality*. It is only such a screening out that lets us imagine we are engaged in objectivity. The text we study and its people, however, will not permit such a screening out and such a self-deception.

The decisive issue may not be "theological protectionism" and "social scientific analysis," but the cruciality of "abiding astonishment" for the sake of humanness, in the present as in the past. In the face of such astonishment, both our "protectionism" and our "analyses" are placed in jeopardy. The question of "what happened" is deeply intertwined in matters of literature, canon, and rhetoric. Speaking in a different context, Andrienne Munich has it right for the history of ancient Israel as well: "The canon has been owned by a monopoly, but the acts of repossession have begun."[117] Those acts of repossession now underway require a different remembering not only *in* Israel, but *of* Israel.

NOTES

BIBLIOGRAPHY

INDEXES

CBQ = *Catholic Biblical Quarterly*
JSOT = *Journal for the Study of the Old Testament*
ZAW = *Zeitschrift für die altestamentliche Wissenschaft*

NOTES

1. Concerning recent discussions of these problems, see J. Maxwell Miller, "Israelite History" (1985:1-30), Robert B. Coote and Keith W. Whitelam, *The Emergence of Early Israel in Historical Perspective* (1987), and John van Seters, *In Search of History* (1983:209-353). For a thoughtful discussion of the problems with a high and conservative view of the "historical" concerns of the biblical tradition, see Baruch Halpern, *The First Historians* (1988).

The entire theme of "theology as recital" was an anticipation of more recent "narrative theology." See G. Ernest Wright, *God Who Acts* (1952), with its subtitle, "Biblical Theology as Recital," and recently Amos Wilder, "Story and Story-World," (1983:353-64).

On the relative significance of what happened and what is remembered, see Yosef Hayim Yerushalmi, *Zakhor: Jewish History and Jewish Memory* (1982). Yerushalmi makes clear the crucial contrast between Jewish modes of "history" and Enlightenment alternatives.

On the "how" of rhetoric in relation to the "what" of substance, see Gail R. O'Day, *Revelation in the Fourth Gospel: Narrative Mode and Theological Claim* (1986:43-8).

2. See Robert Polzin, *Moses and the Deuteronomist* (1980: 1-24), and *Samuel and the Deuteronomist* (1989:1-17). Polzin is more polemical than many other scholars would be, but the substance of his claim represents the state of the methodological turn.

3. Hegel had seen that "history" unites the "objective substance" of events and the subjective narration of those events. That is, "history" covers over the ambiguity between facticity and rhetoric, but the availability of the facts depends on rhetoric. On this programmatic insight of Hegel, see Hayden White, *The Content of Form* (1987:11-7); *Metahistory: The Historical Imagination in Nineteenth Century Europe* (1973:86-98); and Gerda Lerner, *The Creation of Patriarchy* (1986:4 and *passim*).

4. *The Reality of the Historical Past* (1984:4-7), Paul Ricoeur speaks about the interplay of documents, imagination, and reenactment of the past. Even the claims of objective documents depend upon imaginative construction. See the analysis of Stephen Toulmin, *Cosmopolis: The Hidden Agenda of Modernity* (1990:30-35), on the shift toward "objective modes" of historiography.

5. Gerhard von Rad, "The Form-Critical Problem of the Hexateuch" (1966:1-78); *Old Testament Theology I* (1962: 105-305); and George Ernest Wright, *God Who Acts*.

6. On the "core memory," see Walter Harrelson, "Life, Faith, and the Emergence of Tradition" (1977:11-30).

7. The problematic character of such language has been variously commented upon by Langdon Gilkey, "Cosmology, Ontology and the Travail of Biblical Language" (1961:194-205); Gordon P. Kaufman, "On the Memory of 'Act of God'" (1968: 175-201); and James Barr, "Revelation through History in the Old Testament and in Modern Theology" (1963:193-205). The most recent positive review of this language is by Werner E. Lemke, "Revelation through History in Recent Biblical Theo logy" (1982:34-46). On the more general problem, see Owen C. Thomas (ed.), *God's Activity in the World: The Contemporary Problem* (1983), and Maurice Wiles, *God's Action in the World* (1986).

8. See the influential discussion of Van Harvey, *The Historian and the Believer* (1967). J. Alberto Soggin, *A History of Israel* (1984:25-26), is unambiguous on this question. He sets for himself the task of writing a history of Israel in which he programmatically excludes what might be regarded as anything theological: "When we begin to write a history of Israel, we too shall be writing an essentially secular history, a history which therefore leaves out views which Israel had of itself, like 'people of god' or 'elect people'."

9. See van Seters' review of von Rad's work, cited in note 1. Thomas L. Thompson, *The Historicity of the Patriarchal Narratives* (1974) is often linked with van Seters in his review of historical claims made for the Old Testament. Thompson con cludes, "Salvation history is not an historical account of saving events open to the study of the historian. Salvation history did not happen; it is a literary form which has its own historical

context. In fact, we can say that the faith of Israel is not an historical faith, in the sense of a faith based on historical events; it is rather a faith within history" (328). Given his own definitions, Thompson's resolution of the problem is cogent. One might wonder if Thompson acknowledges that his work also "is a literary form which has its own historical context." Everything depends on our paying attention to the fact that every historical account is "a literary rendering" in its own historical context, with its own sociological interest.

10. On the literary form of these Psalms of recital, see Erhard Gerstenberger, "The Psalms" (1974:212-214).

11. Of the others, Psalm 135 might well be included. My argument, however, is not effected by the inclusion or exclusion of other examples. I have proceeded to make my argument in reference to the clearest examples.

12. Von Rad, "Problem" (1966:53).

13. On this Psalm and the cruciality of this word, see Gary A. Herion, "The Role of Historical Narrative in Biblical Thought: The Tendencies Underlying Old Testament Historiography" (1981:41).

14. Herion (37-42).

15. In *Israel's Praise* (1988:74-87), I have suggested the way in which the Psalms are "formed up" from specificity to generalization, even though we have learned to "sing down" in the inverse order.

16. See A. F. Campbell, "Psalm 78: A Contribution to the Theology of Tenth Century Israel" (1979:51-79), and Richard J. Clifford, "In Zion and David a New Beginning: An Interpretation of Psalm 78" (1981:121-41).

17. See Walter Brueggemann, "When Jerusalem Gloats Over Shiloh" (1990:24-7), for a contemporary interface with this text.

18. See Brueggemann, *Israel's Praise*, chapter 1. See Wilder, "Story and Story-World" (1983:353-64).

19. This affirmation is challenged by the argument of Jer 31:29-30, and Ezek 18:3-4. Both those cases challenge the proverbial saying. In these recitals of the Psalms, however, the proverbial saying is assumed and not challenged. See the peculiar connection between past and present generations in Hebrews 11:39-40. The actions of the present generation

determine the "perfection" of the past generations. This thesis reverses the claim of the proverb, but continues to link the generations in crucial ways. See the thoughtful and persuasive discussion of these texts by Paul Joyce, *Divine Initiative and Human Response in Ezekiel* (1989:33-60).

20. On this mutual binding as definitional for Israel, see Rudolf Smend, *Die Bundesformel* (1963) and Gerd Theissen, *Biblical Faith* (1983).

21. The assertion that history in Israel is an on-going narrative account is of crucial importance for my argument, even though it might seem to be obvious and common-place. In this statement, I intend to draw together (a) the argument of Hayden White in "The Historical Text as Literary Artifact" (1978:44-61), *Metahistory* (1975), and "Rhetoric and History" (1978:3-25), that *history is essentially narrative rendering*; (b) the insistence of W. B. Gallie in *Philosophy and the Historical Understanding* (1964:22-104), that *narrative is a different mode of argument* which requires a different way of appropriation, and (c) the assertion of George A. Lindbeck in *The Nature of Doctrine* (1984), that a *community must be granted its own modes of articulation*. The convergence of the insights of White, Gallie, and Lindbeck are of great importance for current issues concerning history *in* Israel and history *of* Israel.

22. That moral decisiveness in the end leads to the recognition that *deeds* have serious, non-negotiable *consequences*. Klaus Koch, in "Is there a Doctrine of Retribution in the Old Testament?" (1983:57-87), has programmatically explored two different systems of moral discourse in ancient Israel, one depending on divine intervention, the other operating according to its own "spheres of destiny." See Brueggemann, "A Shape for Old Testament Theology, I: Structure Legitimation" (1985: 28-46).

23. The possibility of newness asserts that a system of "deeds-consequences" does not ultimately prevail against the power of Yahweh's yearning fidelity. In crucial ways, yearning overrides the power of "deeds-consequences." See Brueggemann, "A Shape for Old Testament Theology, II: Embrace of Pain" (1985:395-415).

24. On the continuation and lack of closure to the conversation, George Steiner, in *Real Presences* (1989), asserts: "It is

the Hebraic intuition that God is capable of all speech-acts except that of monologue which has generated our arts of reply, of questioning, and counter-creation. After the Book of Job and Euripides' *Bacchae*, there *had* to be, if man was to bear his being, the means of dialogue with God which are spelt out in our poetics, music, art" (225). It is this open commitment to dialogue that we are witnessing in these Psalms of recital. Harold Fisch, in *Poetry with a Purpose* (1988:118), refers to such poetry as "covenantal discourse."

25. In *Lectures on Ideology and Utopia* (1986), Paul Ricoeur has helpfully probed the various positive and negative functions of "ideology." I suggest, in Ricoeur's terms, that Israel's old recital offers a "constitutive ideology." Psalm 78, with its Davidic departure from the old recital, may be variously read as a distortion or as a constitution for a new social possibility. Here I assume the first assessment, i.e., that Psalm 78 is a distortion of the old constitutive ideology.

26. Ricoeur (1986:173-82) shrewdly sees that utopian thought is an enquiry into power and a challenge to present forms of power. In that sense, these Psalms or recitals are utopian. Ricoeur observes that utopian literature has the intention of "redescribing life" (309-10).

27. On one assessment of the political interest at work in the north-south controversy, see Martin A. Cohen, "The Role of the Shilonite Priesthood in the United Monarchy of Ancient Israel" (1965:59-98).

28. On this tension programmatically considered, see Eric Voegelin, *Order and History* (1956), and Paul Van Buren, *A Theology of the Jewish-Christian Reality II* (1983:184-9). On Voegelin's work, see the acute analysis by Bernhard W. Anderson, "Politics and the Transcendent: Voegelin's Philosophical and Theological Exposition of the Old Testament in the Context of the Ancient Near East" (1978:62-100).

29. On praise as polemic, see James L. Mays, "Worship, World, and Power" (1969:315-30).

30. In *Israel's Praise* (1988:89-121), I have characterized these seductions and dangers as idolatry (false discernment of God) and ideology (false articulation of social reality). On the juxtaposition of idolatry and ideology, see W. J. T. Mitchell,

Iconology: Image, Text, Ideology (1986:38, 113-115, 151, 164, and *passim*).

31. Emil Fackenheim, in *God's Presence in History* (1970), has explored the dialectic of past and present in Israel's mode of remembering. More concretely, Michael Fishbane, in *Text and Texture* (1979:79-83), suggests that Deut 6:20-25 reflects the resistance of the new generation to the discernments and convictions of the old generation, thereby also rejecting the normative character of the experience of the older generation.

32. See Abraham J. Heschel, *Who is Man?* (1965:83-5 and *passim*), and Gregory Baum, *Theology and Society* (1987:51).

33. A rabbi, commenting on the holocaust, recently asserted, "At Auschwitz, all ten commandments were systematically violated. And whenever all ten commandments are systematically violated, the outcome will inevitably be Auschwitz."

34. See Brueggemann, *Hope Within History* (1987:49-71). To stop the conversation misunderstands both the character and will of God, and the nature of the human process. Thus it will not do for the powerful, in heaven or on earth, to stop speech from below for the sake of a monologue of power.

35. Wilder, "Story and Story-World" has seen that stories are indeed the makers of "home." The absence of story produces homelessness. See the analysis of modern homelessness by Peter Berger, Brigitte Berger, and Hansfried Kellner, *The Homeless Mind* (1974).

36. This peculiar Jewish reality has been poignantly explicated by Cynthia Ozick, *Metaphor and Memory* (1989:265-283).

37. On rhetoric as the inescapable sphere of history, see White, "Rhetoric and History" (1978:3-25). See also "The Historical Text" (1978:57), where he asserts, "Historians constitute by the very language they use to describe." Israel is uncompromising in its insistence on its language for constitution. Notice Ricoeur, *Lectures* (1986), argues that ideology "constitutes." Thus *rhetoric*, as in these Psalms, is the practice of *constituting ideology*.

38. See Brueggemann, *Hope Within History* (1987:49-71), and "Old Testament Theology as a Particular Conversation: Adjudication of Israel's Socio-theological Alternatives" (1985: 303-25).

39. See Brueggemann, " 'Impossibility' and Epistemology in the Faith Traditions of Abraham and Sarah (Genesis 18: 1-15)" (1982:615-34).

40. Martin Buber, *Moses* (1946 [1988]:75-76; the italics are added).

41. Von Rad regularly refers to this old and stylized recital as "canonical," meaning that it becomes normative for all subsequent reflection. Cf. von Rad, *Old Testament Theology I* (1982:129 and *passim*). This dynamic sense of canon is what is intended by Garrett Green, *Imagining God* (1989:113, 124-5 and *passim*), when he refers to the "canon" as the model, paradigm, or pattern of subsequent reflection and interpretation.

42. Buber, *Moses* (1946:76). See the cruciality of this claim as understood by Ozick (1989:n.39). Ozick urges that it is the Exodus narrative, the same one so crucial for Buber, that gives Jewishness its distinctive humane power.

43. Buber, *Moses* (1946:77).

44. See for example Alan Richardson, *History Sacred and Profane* (1964). See the comments on Richardson by Van Harvey, *The Historian and the Believer* (230-4).

45. Emil Fackenheim, *God's Presence in History* (1972: 8-14).

46. Fackenheim (9-10).

47. Fackenheim (13-4).

48. The dynamic and decisive connection between past memory and present discernment and practice are at the heart of the analysis of Yerushalmi. It is clear that our modern modes of "history" operate from a set of assumptions completely discontinuous from this dynamic.

49. The monarchal period surely was a time of less availability and less credibility for such original claims. There is little doubt that von Rad is correct in his proposal that the Davidic-Solomonic period was a time of an epistemological revolution in Israel. Cf. *Old Testament Theology I* (1982:48-55, 140-41, 425-29). Crenshaw's strictures against the hypothesis of the Enlightenment require that the matter be stated more precisely, but Crenshaw's arguments do not, in my judgment, nullify von Rad's point. See van Seters, *In Search of History* (1983:216-20),

and Brueggemann, "Solomon as Patron of Wisdom" (forthcoming).

50. James Barr, *The Scope and Authority of the Bible* (1980:36), has argued that these primal acts are not to be construed factually, but rather are offered to function as "paradigms" for on-going historical experience and interpretation.

51. On the shift of interpretive presuppositions among modern historians, see the suggestive essay of Lionel Gossman, "History and Literature" (1978:3-39). The shift from portrayal to description, from "rhetoric" to "facts," was intended as a move toward "objectivity." It was in fact a shift in the form of rhetoric which redefined the perimeters of acceptable "fact." Gossman's essay makes clear that the embrace of "objectivity" was much less ambiguous than warranted, and entailed important costs as well as gains. Richard Rorty, in *Philosophy and the Mirror of Nature* (1980:335), characterizes "objective" as "never anything more than an expression of the presence of, or the hope for, agreement among inquirers.

52. Donald P. Spence, in *Narrative Truth and Historical Truth* (1982:24-27 and *passim*), has explored the dialectic of truth in psycho-therapy as it moves to truth "inside the hour" and truth "outside the hour." That is, "inside the hour" of the therapeutic conversation, certain truth claims are made that belong to the perceptual field and constructive apparatus of the analysand. The truth claims "inside the hour" have a different quality from what may be regarded as "reality" outside the hour of therapeutic conversation. We are coming to see, however, that the truth claims inside the hour have a certain kind of privilege, if the conversation is to nurture healing. To assess such truth claims by "reality" elsewhere may be more "scientific," but of doubtful value for the reality of healing. This very difficult issue has been explored by George K. Ganaway in "Exploring the Credibility Issue in Multiple Personality Disorder and Related Dissociative Phenomena" (1989). I am grateful to Catherine Taylor for this reference. This model for psychotherapy is useful to us in our concern about historical recital. It warns us that our attempt to get at "historical truth" "outside the hour" is more perilous than our scientific methods may suggest. Spence argues that the truth "inside the hour" must be taken with utmost seriousness.

53. On "reconstruction" see Soggin (1984:20), where he speaks of "an authentic and normative reconstruction of events," and John H. Hayes and J. Maxwell Miller, *Israelite and Judean History* (1977:65-6).

54. Burke O. Long, "The Social World of Ancient Israel" (1982:244). I have found Long's statement a helpful one with which to engage. While I have taken issue with his argument, I do so only because his article is enormously clarifying. I suspect that in more recent development, Long and I would not greatly differ. In any case, I am grateful to him for the clarity and carefulness of his argument.

55. Soggin speaks of the danger of "contamination" caused by imagination. Soggin employs the word "contamination" as "legal jargon" (1984:20). One may of course wonder if the metaphor of "detective" as used by Soggin is at all applicable to the reconstructive work of the historian. On such a decontaminated program, Annette Kolodny, in "Dancing Through the Minefield" (1985:163), asserts: "If feminist criticism calls anything into question, it must be that god-eared myth of intellectual neutrality."

56. In his commentary on I Samuel (1980), P. Kyle Mc-Carter, Jr. characteristically regards theological judgments in the narrative as late intrusions which interrupt the historical narrative. The criteria for such a distinction are, in my judgment, scarcely objective, but reflect an assumption about a certain kind of historicality in the narrative.

57. Assessing contemporary "pastoral care," Thomas Odin, in *Care of Souls in the Classic Tradition* (1984), has traced the way in which there has been a complete change of references from theological to modern-scientific perspectives. His critique is that such a change of references has distorted the work of pastoral care. It may well be that a comparable "change of references" has taken place in "scientific" efforts at Israel's history that distort the character of that history.

58. On writing as a criterion for "history" see van Seters, *In Search of History* (1983:1-7), and William W. Hallo, "Biblical History in its Near Eastern Setting" (1980:9-11). While enormous attention has been given to the early poetry, especially by Cross and Freedman, that interest has focused on linguistic structure and dating, without any serious recognition that the

rhetoric of these poems is a rendering of "what happened." The poems mean to assert that this is indeed "what happened."

After I had compiled my list of five factors characterizing the historiographic warrants of modernity, I saw Toulmin's trenchant analysis in *Cosmopolis* (1990:30-5, 186-92). While there is important overlap in my statement and his, my own is independent of his and could well be modified in light of his analysis. I am grateful to Brian Childs for the reference to Toulmin.

59. In using the word "real" in this way, I deliberately take up the use of Burke Long, but in an opposite way. Long uses "real" in quotes to refer to what lies beyond the limits of the natural and social order of human experience. Long's use of quotes clearly intends to make an epistemological distinction, as well as a judgment about what in fact is reality.

Attention, however, should be paid to Peter Berger's observation that sociologists always work with quotation marks. Thus there still remains the interpretive question about which reality should be placed in quotation marks. Those who champion "objective history" place theological claims in quotes, but the reverse is also possible; from a certain rhetorical perspective, the claims of "objectivity" can also be placed in quotes. It is not neutrally obvious but always interpretive to decide which claim is *real* and which is "real."

60. On the notion of "state truth," see M. I. Steblin-Kamenskij, *The Saga Mind* (1973).

61. On the deception of "objectivity," see the essays of Gossman and White in *The Writing of History*, cited above (notes 17 and 37). On the deadening effect of such "objective" language, see Geoffrey H. Hartman, *Saving the Text: Literature Derrida, Philosophy* (1981) where he writes, "Words have been found that close the path to the original words. This absolute closure is what we respond to, this appearance of definitive detachment and substitute. The words themselves block the way." He concludes, "The 'dread voice' exists as the poem or not at all."

62. On the matter of human initiative, see the wondrous aphorism of Clare Booth Luce: "History has no time for more than one sentence, and it is always a sentence that has an active verb," *Time Magazine* (Oct. 19, 1987:32). Luce, of course, would interpret history in terms of human initiative and

human control. It matters for interpretation who are assumed to be the subjects of the one active verb.

63. Ricoeur,in his *Lectures* (1986), makes a helpful distinction in assessing economic "causes." He opines that economic influence can be understood only in terms of "motivation," not as mechanical cause and effect. A mechanistic notion of cause and effect is not helpful in understanding the historical process, nor does it reflect on how history works. In this important distinction, Ricoeur follows Edmund Husserl's essay "Essential Distinctions" (1986:169): ". . . in perceiving something as 'motivated' we are not at all perceiving it as caused."

64. The phrase "theological protectionism" is from Long (248).

65. Howard Zinn, in *A People's History of the United States* (1980:9), attributes this statement to Kissinger: "History is the memory of states." Zinn cites Kissinger's book, *A World Restored* (1973), but gives no page reference.

In *Salvation and Liberation*, Leonardo & Clodovis Boff comment on the ideological force of "the winners": ". . . the ideology of the dominant classes who have 'made it to the top' and who have done away with memory in the vanquished. That is, the winners have killed memory in the losers, so that now everyone's consciousness of history is that of the victors"(1984: 28-9). Jo Anne Engelbert, in her "Introduction" to *And We Sold the Rain*, writes:

> Occasionally this amputation of history, coupled with a rigid censorship was successful in colonizing the imagination . . . Against the powerful ideologies imposing themselves in the isthmus, the ancient strategies of the embattled storyteller— parable and allegory, parody and satire, fable and fantastic tale—were in colonial times, as now, invaluable arms in the struggle to ransom the abducted past, to delineate and to denounce a repressive present. (1988:xiii-xiv)

The phrases, "colonizing the imagination," "ancient strategies," and "ransom the abducted past," speak directly to the suffocating power of dominant ideology and the frail but resilient counters to it.

66. Ronald Reagan, disturbed that focus was on a concrete crisis rather than on the center of power in Washington,

demanded, "Is it news that some fellow out in South Succotash has just been laid off?" (Cf. *Time*, March 29, 1982:27)

67. See Brueggemann, "The Rhetoric of Hurt and Hope: Ethics Odd and Crucial" (1989:73-92). Lamentably, much of the current discussion of ethics in parallel fashion prefers rationalistic categories to the elemental matters of human hurt and human hope.

68. Fully congruent with von Ranke's program, the pursuit of "objectivity" seeks to disclose what was "there", "as it really happened." Such an ambition is the counterpart of Soggin's notion of avoiding "contamination." For an extreme expression of the pursuit of "objectivity" that is free of "ideology," see Giovanni Garbini, *History and Ideology in Ancient Israel* (1988).

69. What emerges is "objective reconstruction," which clearly is an oxymoron. One cannot have it both ways. The initial hope of objectivity did not intend to "reconstruct," but to "report" and "describe." Once it is conceded that the historian "reconstructs," the claim of "objectivity" is exceedingly problematic. Alasdair MacIntyre, in *Whose Justice? Which Rationality?* (1988:326-48), has shown how even the tradition of liberalism, which purports to be objective and rational, is a contextualized tradition that can be criticized. Such "objectivity" does not stand outside or above the practice of criticism, because it also is socially embedded.

70. Ricoeur, in his *Lectures* (1986), characterizes "utopia" as thought which rethinks and redescribes, and which challenges what is. In this sense, objective reconstruction is an antithesis to utopia, and belongs on the side of ideology which, with Ricoeur, may be constitutive or distorting.

71. Objective modernity wants to eliminate Yahweh as a key actor in the historical process. It is fair to assume that the ancient monopolists also wanted to eliminate Yahweh as a key actor in the historical process, if indeed Yahweh was a liberating force allied with the marginal. The elimination of Yahweh as a key actor may be done by nullifying the category "god" from historical understanding (as in modern objectiveness), or by retaining the category Yahweh but domesticating Yahwism to fit the reasons of the state. The ancient and modern eliminations

of "god" are not very different in their intents or in their consequences.

72. See the discerning comments of Herion (25-57), and especially his reference to Robert Redfield's "The Social Organization of Tradition" (1967). The contrast of "little story" and "great story" is crucial for Herion's analysis and for my argument. My general question concerns how the "little story" is to be honored in historical reconstruction, if it is cast in "the wrong mode," that is, as rhetoric that lacks both the claim of objectivity and the legitimacy of the dominant rhetoric.

73. Soggin understands the task to be the writing of "secular history." One wonders whether his or any other conventional rendering is not only secular but "from above." It is no more than a play on words, but it is interesting that the titles of Soggin's last chapters (XII, XIII, XIV) all begin with "under"! Soggin's view of history, objectively reconstructed, is "from above" and views Israel as "under." The methods of so-called objectivity preclude any other mapping.

74. "Secular" reconstructions tend not only to eliminate "God" from Israel's memory, but also to silence dangerous human speech. Since dangerous speech is the main social power of the powerless and the main social threat against established, monopolized power, "free speech" is always a threat to established power. Israel's mode of remembered rhetoric is thus not simply a manner of remembering, but also a particular way of addressing established power in the present. When this odd rhetoric is silenced, established power is that much more secure.

75. The power and dominance of such "rational objectivity" is increasingly open to critical suspicion. In addition to Stephen Toulmin's *Cosmopolis*, see Susan Bordo, *The Flight to Objectivity*, wherein Bordo suggests that the appeal of objectivity is a response to a cosmic sense of abandonment, that is, an attempt to produce order, security, and finally control.

76. My argument that "salvation history" is a counter-history as reaction against imperial ("scientific") history is parallel to the sociological argument of Norman K. Gottwald, in *The Tribes of Yahweh* (1979), that tribal community is a reaction against the power of the state. In both cases, the conventional evolutionary assumption is turned on its head. It is our

usual assumption that state follows tribe. In parallel fashion, it is our usual assumption that "secular" history comes after "salvation history." I suggest that sociological realism might permit a reversal of this sequence. As Gottwald has suggested that tribe may be a protest against state, so I suggest that a historical recital of "astonishment" may be a protest against too many imperial "facts."

77. The general problem of a sociology of knowledge is thus posed. Those "underneath" must necessarily "know" in a very different way. This knowing may come in "acting justly" (cf. Jer. 22:16), or in praising. On praising, see Daniel N. Hardy and David F. Ford, *Praising and Knowing God* (1985). Such counter-modes of knowledge, perhaps congruent with recent interpretation of the verb "know" (*yd'*) as "covenantal loyalty," are quite in contrast to the autonomous modes of scientific and imperial knowledge. If this "knowing" is a counter-confession against royal, scientific rationality, we can understand why Hosea and Jeremiah polemize against a people that does "not know." Hans Walter Wolff, in "'Wissen um Gott' bei Hosea als Urform von Theologie" (1964:182-205), has suggested that the substance of such "knowledge of God" is precisely the recital of the saving tradition.

78. Hayden White, in *The Content of the Form* (1987: 13-25), argues persuasively that historical narrative, because it is narrative, serves to articulate moral awareness and moral authority. Israel's rhetoric thus asserts a moral shape to its memory, a moral shape which is crucial to the narrator, and which is abandoned when the rhetoric is discarded.

79. Long (248) makes the contrast in a way that appears either to dismiss or polemize against theological claims.

80. I pose the question about historicality in the Bible by drawing analogies from contemporary situations of oppression. Any argument from contemporary analogy is of course problematic. I am, however, not posing questions about ancient texts, but about contemporary scholarly presuppositions. On that ground, I take the analogies to be pertinent. Examples of "counter-data" outside the "memory of the state" include Adam Michnich, *Letters from Prison and Other Essays* (1985) in Poland, Andre Brink, *A Dry White Season* (1979), *A Chain of Voices* (1983), and Nadine Gordimer, *A Sport of Nature* (1987)

in South Africa. On varieties of academic feminism, see *Making a Difference* (1985). In this volume, Sydney Janet Kaplan raises the crucial question, " . . . who establishes the literary canon and *whose* interests it serves" ("Varieties of Feminist Criticism," 41).

81. Thus in section VI I have been concerned with history "from above" and "from below." In this section I will consider history "from the insider" and history "from the outsider."

82. The practical effect of such acceptability and credibility is that the Psalms lie (by their half truth) in bracketing out the justice questions, in pretending there are no raging, unresolved issues of theodicy. The memory and literature which protest against such a canonical denial and "cover-up" is parallel to the work of women's history as recognized by Elizabeth Fox-Genovese, "Placing Women's History in History" (1982:28). Fox-Genovese writes: ". . . women's history challenges mainstream history not to substitute the chronicle of the female subject for that of the male, but rather to restore conflict, ambiguity and tragedy to the centre of historical process." See the comments on Fox-Genovese's program by Gayle Greene and Coppela Kahn in "Feminist Scholarship and the Social Construction of Woman" (1985:21).

In Israel, the literature "underneath" also seeks to restore "conflict, ambiguity, and tragedy," which has been expelled by the dominant historical rendering, "to the centre of the historical process." Commenting on the subversive intention of early women's novels, Sandra M. Gilbert and Susan Gubar, in *The Madwoman in the Attic* (1979:85), conclude of such authors, "They expressed their claustrophobic rage by enacting rebellious escapes." I submit that the literature of Israel from below, in a very different mode, enacted the same kind of "rebellious escapes." This rhetoric from below wants to restore "conflict, ambiguity, and tragedy to the center of the historical process." Thus the "official" program that "God acts" does not acknowledge the painful social outcome when God does not act. On the pathos of this unresolve, see IV Ezra 7-8 and *passim*. History writing thus may be a proposed theodicy, with either a stable settlement or a troubled crisis. Peter Berger, in *The Sacred Canopy* (1969:57-63, has observed the fact that these two theodicies can exist along side each other. My argument here is that the stronger theodicy, as reflected in these "canonical" Psalms, tends to censor, silence, and eliminate the weaker one by its self-legitimating and, I dare say, self-serving claims.

83. Herion (1981:40-2) sees Psalm 105 (in contrast to Micah 6) as a settlement "from above."

84. John Goldingay, "The Dynamic Cycle of Praise and Prayer in the Psalms" (1981:85-90).

85. The most spectacular case is that of Alex Haley, *Roots* (1976). On a much more modest scale, see Barbara Brown Zikmund (editor), *Hidden Histories in the United Church of Christ* (1984:1-2). A spectacular case of such history being hidden is articulated by Virginia Woolf, *A Room of One's Own* (1929:134-6 and *passim*). Woolf writes:

> All these infinitely obscure lives remain to be recorded . . . feeling in imagination the pressure of dumbness, the accumulation of unrecorded life . . . and there is a girl behind the counter too—I would as soon have her true history as the hundred and fiftieth life of Napoleon or seventeenth study of Keats and his use of Miltonic inversion which old Professor Z and his like are now inditing." (93-94)

86. The voiceless, when they claim voice, are the "voice of illness" yearning for health. A. Siraala, in *The Voice of Illness* (1964), has provided a suggestive analysis, showing that the very sounding of illness is an insistence on health. What Siraala has seen about the function of the body, Erhard Gerstenberger, in "Der klagende Mensch" (1971:64-72), has seen in parallel fashion about the Psalms. He observes that the complaint Psalms are in fact a voice of hope. In the larger canon of ancient Israel, that is, beyond the scope of the Psalms of historical recital, the voices of marginality press to be included in Israel's narrative recital. On the powerful healing that happens when the voiceless find voice, see Howard Brody, *Stories of Sickness* (1987), and A. Kleinman, *The Illness Narratives* (1988).

87. On the power of the canon, see Elizabeth A. Meese, "Sexual Politics and Critical Judgment" (1985:85-100). Note especially her quote of Kolodny (90).

In a variety of places, Frank Kermode converts the question "What is great literature?" into the question of canon. Thus in a different context, Kermode is exploring what constitutes "the great story" in the midst of "little stories" that keep impinging upon it.

88. The shift in interpretive awareness proceeds on two principles. First, interpretation is *pluralistic*. There are varieties of texts which are not homogeneous, and there are varieties of interpreters who do not share a common perspective. They cannot be forced into a single harmonious ideational scheme. Second, interpretation is always *contextual*, and therefore local. There is no contextless (presuppositionless, objective) interpretation, and no global stance that transcends partial and partisan interest. The objectivist assumption believes it can overcome both pluralism and contextualism, failing to see that objectivism is also a partial, partisan practice. Robert J. Schreiter, in *Constructing Local Theologies* (1985:31-8), has shown how all theology is, at root, local theology.

89. Phyllis Trible, *Texts of Terror* (1984). The literature generated around this concern is extensive and burgeoning. The collection of essays edited by Peggy L. Day, *Gender and Difference in Ancient Israel* (1989), is representative of the emerging literature, includes some of the most important contributors to the discussion, and offers extensive bibliography.

90. Among the voices of memory not censored or eliminated are voices of grief, rage, guilt, and gratitude. These are not by definition inimical to the narrative recital. When given personal, local, intimate articulation, however, they are a practice of "little story" that does not easily conform to the great recital. Specifically the individual song of thanksgiving gives a very different texture to memory and recital than does the great narrative recital. Cf. Rainer Albertz, *Persönliche Frömmigkeit und offizielle Religion* (1978), and Peter Doll, *Menschenschöpfung und Weltschöpfung in der alttestamentliche Weisheit* (1985). It may be pressing too far, but it is suggestive to think that the "great recital" is characteristically patriarchal, while the more localized voices are maternal.

91. The communal recital is not false in what it asserts, but in what it fails to mention. In the royal genealogy of Matthew, some of the marginalized women of Israel have finally gained their way into the normative recital (Matt. 1:3-6). In parallel fashion, women are pushing their way into the literary canon of the academy. See the trenchant criticism of Kolodny, in "A Map

of Reading" (1985:46-62), on resistance of the dominant canon to new literature from below.

92. See Gustavo Gutierrez's *On Job* (1987) for an exploration of the voice of the innocent who have nothing of which to repent, but who are victims of social arrangements of injustice.

93. See Brueggemann, "Theodicy in a Social Dimension" (1985:3-25).

94. This theodicy is a full and confident acceptance of a theory of "deeds-consequences." See Klaus Koch, "Is there a Doctrine of Retribution in the Old Testament?" (1983:57-87). In *The Message of the Psalms* (1984:25-8, 168-76), I have dealt with this theodic settlement under the rubric of "The Psalms of Orientation."

95. See James L. Crenshaw, *Whirlpool of Torment* (1984: 57-92).

96. On the theme of presence, perhaps the most important and subtle text is Exodus 32-34. On this text, see the perceptive discussion of R. Walter L. Moberly, *At the Mountain of God* (1983).

97. See Robert N. Bellah, "Biblical Religion and Social Science in the Modern World" (1982:8-22).

98. On this tension of waiting and acting, see Christoph Blumhardt's formulation in Karl Barth, *Action in Waiting* (1969:42 and *passim*).

99. The programmatic work of Claus Westermann and especially the series of studies by Erhard Gerstenberger do nonetheless represent a significant effort to keep the rhetoric of dissent operative amidst focus on "the mighty deeds." This literature of dissent is, as Gerstenberger has shown, an act of hope, because it insists that the God who has not acted "for us" can and must act. Thus the dissent from marginality has nothing in common with modernity which precludes God's action. On the contrary it insists on God acting.

100. Current interest in the wisdom tradition surely reflects the general situation of Western culture and the epistemological stance of the scholars who pursue it. That is, the vitality of current wisdom studies is not merely an academic matter, but needs to be understood in terms of the context and sociology of

the interpreters. In this connection, the work of Crenshaw is representative and especially important.

101. The rejection of this rhetoric comes from those who have escaped the community by climbing out "on top," not from those who have fallen out of the community from the bottom.

102. The rhetoric of Israel's memory does not tell simply "what happened," but offers a paradigm for the present. The paradigm is offered with linguistic particularity and construes the past with a certain moral shape. Concerning paradigmatic presentation, see Voegelin, *Israel and Revelation* (1956:121-2 and *passim*). Concerning linguistic particularity, see MacIntyre, *Whose Justice? Which Rationality?* (1988:9 and *passim*). Concerning moral construal of the past, see White, *The Content of the Form* (1987:13-25).

103. By the phrase "royal history" I mean the presentation of the history of ancient Israel as being coterminous with the origins of the state. Currently there is an inclination to conclude that nothing is recoverable before the appearance of the state, which then becomes the beginning point for "the history of Israel." Such a royal rendering of Israel is clearly against the grain of the data itself and reflects the perceptive lens of the scholars who adjudicate matters in this way. That is, much of current historiography is prepared to view the problem of history through a royal lens which permits only certain kinds of data to register. This is not a disinterested inclination, but likely reflects the social location of those who "reconstruct."

104. I do not shrink from calling this historical self-understanding and self-presentation "ideological," as long as "ideology" is understood as a proposal of a meaning structure. Moreover the critical dismissal of this "ideology" is not ever done in the interest of neutrality, but in the service of a counter-ideology, which sometimes is the counter-ideology of "objectivity."

105. The "abiding astonishment" reflected in the historical recitals is not simply an experience of religious transcendentalism; it is dazzlement that the holy power of God subverts, inverts, and transforms public power arrangements. Thus, I suggest, that the recitals, both in their content and casting, are inherently subversive of all established power. The reason is

that the recitals posit, confess, name, and testify to an agent who lies outside present power arrangements and is undomesticated by them. It is this one named in the recital who is the subject of the recital and who is the hope embedded in Israel's memory. In naming this agent who produces "abiding astonishment," Israel's recital deabsolutizes every other pretender to historical power and authority.

106. Buber, in *Kingship of God* (1967:108-62), has seen the political dimension of the claim of Sinai which has now been variously treated by George Mendenhall (*Law and Covenant in Israel and the Ancient Near East* [1955], *The Tenth Generation* [1973], and "The Conflict Between Value Systems and Social Control" [1975:169-80]), and by Norman K. Gottwald (*The Tribes of Yahweh* [1979:642-9, 692-709, and *passim*]). It is through this language that Gottwald reclaims Yahweh to be a "function" of social revolution.

107. Concerning the "end result" of Israel's self-presentation, see the claim of Josh. 21:43-45. Von Rad, in "The Form-Critical Problem of the Hexateuch" (1966:71-8), has seen how the narrative moves to "the settlement." The traditioning generation regarded itself as the "end result," to whom all the promises had been kept.

108. On the exclusion of the marginal, see Gerda Lerner, *The Creation of Patriarchy* (1986). Lerner makes an important distinction between "history" which is unrecorded past and "History" which is recorded and interpreted past (4). It is in the latter that ideological exclusion is enacted. Thus the marginal are present in "history" but excluded from "History." In my discussion of marginality, I have been especially informed by literature concerning the exclusion of women because that exclusion is so poignant, so available, and so powerfully illustrative of the larger issue of exclusivism.

109. On the Kantian and Marxian dimensions of the Enlightenment, see Paul Connenton, *The Tragedy of Enlightenment* (1980), John B. Thompson, *Critical Hermeneutics* (1981), and Max Horkheimer and T. W. Adorno, *Dialectic of Enlightenment* (1972). I am grateful to M. Douglas Meeks for these references and for my understanding of these issues.

110. G. Ernest Wright, *Biblical Archeology* (1957:65).

111. There is some irony in Wright's sort of judgment cited above, because such a comment, as "explanation," is in deep tension with Wright's magisterial insistence on a "God who acts." Wright's archaeological conclusion rejects the rhetoric of a "God who acts" and in fact expels God from the "wonder."

112. On the self-deception of such rationalizing, see Herbert W. Schneidau, "Biblical Narrative and Modern Consciousness" (1986:132-50).

113. Michael A. Arbib and Mary B. Hesse, in *The Construction of Reality* (1986:151 and *passim*), speak of "family resemblances" in language. The rhetoric of ancient Israel is situated in such a family orbit of language and cannot be removed from that linguistic network. See also MacIntyre (1988). Clodovis Boff, in "The Poor of Latin America and Their New Ways of Liberation" (1987:33-44), characterizes an alternative mode of participation in the historical process.

114. Notice that this function of rhetoric applies to history *in* Israel. It does not apply to history *of* Israel as conventionally construed. We are required then to ask about the legitimacy of a history *of* Israel that moves a great distance away from the rhetoric of history *in* Israel. The further historical reconstruction "of" moves away from history "in," the less it is in contact with the subject it purports to characterize.

115. Michael Walzer, *Exodus and Revolution* (1985). See also the collection of essays in *Exodus—A Lasting Paradigm* (1987).

116. Schneidau, "Let the Reader Understand" (1987: 140-1). We need not adjudicate Schneidau's claim that Israel is the first to express such a concern. It is enough to notice that such a concern is a characteristic and recurring theme in Israel, regardless of what may have transpired elsewhere, before or after.

117. Adrienne Munich, "Notorious Songs: Feminist Criticism and Literary Tradition" (in Green & Kahn, 1985:257).

BIBLIOGRAPHY

Albertz, Rainer. 1978. *Persönliche Frömmigkeit und offizielle Religion.* Calwer Theologische Monographien 9. Stuttgart: Calwer.

Anderson, Bernhard W. 1978. "Politics and the Transcendent: Voegelin's Philosophical and Theological Exposition of the Old Testament in the Context of the Ancient Near East." In *Eric Voegelin's Search for Order in History.* Stephen A. McKnight, ed. Baton Rouge: Louisiana State Univ. Pp. 62-100.

Arbib, Michael A. and Mary B. Hesse. 1986. *The Construction of Reality.* Cambridge: Cambridge Univ.

Barr, James. 1963. "Revelation through History in the Old Testament and in Modern Theology." *Interpretation* 17:193-205.

———. 1980. *The Scope and Authority of the Bible.* Explorations in Theology 7. London: SCM.

Barth, Karl. 1969. *Action and Waiting.* Rifton, NY: Plough Pub. House.

Baum, Gregory. 1987. *Theology and Society.* New York: Paulist.

Bellah, Robert N. 1982. "Biblical Religion and Social Science in the Modern World." *NICM Journal for Jews and Christians in Higher Education* 63:8-22.

Berger, Peter. 1969. *The Sacred Canopy.* Anchor Books. Garden City: Doubleday.

Berger, Peter, Brigitte Berger and Hansfried Kellner. 1974. *The Homeless Mind: Modernization and Consciousness.* New York: Vintage.

Boff, Clodovis. 1987. "The Poor of Latin America and Their New Ways of Liberation." In *Changing Values and Virtues.* Dietmar Mieth and Jacques Pohier, eds. Concilium 191. Edinburgh: T&T Clark. Pp. 33-44.

Boff, Leonardo and Clodovis. 1984. *Salvation and Liberation.* Maryknoll: Orbis.

Bordo, Susan R. 1987. *The Flight to Objectivity: Essays in Cartesianism and Culture.*

Brink, Andre. 1979. *A Dry White Season.* New York: Penguin.

———. 1983. *A Chain of Voices.* New York: Penguin.

Brody, Howard. 1987. *Stories of Sickness.* New Haven: Yale Univ.

Brueggemann, Walter. 1982. "'Impossibility' and Epistemology in the Faith Traditions of Abraham and Sarah (Genesis 18:1-15)." *ZAW* 94:615-34.

———. 1984. *The Message of the Psalms.* Minneapolis: Augsburg.

———. 1985. "Theodicy in a Social Dimension." *JSOT* 33:3-25.

——. 1985. "A Shape for Old Testament Theology, II: Embrace of Pain." *CBQ* 47:395-415.

——. 1985. "A Shape for Old Testament Theology, I: Structure Legitimation." *CBQ* 47:28-46.

——. 1985. "Old Testament Theology as a Particular Conversation: Adjudication of Israel's Socio-theological Alternatives." *Theology Digest* 32:303-25.

——. 1987. *Hope Within History.* Atlanta: John Knox.

——. 1988. *Israel's Praise: Doxology Against Idolatry and Ideology.* Philadelphia: Fortress.

——. 1989. "The Rhetoric of Hurt and Hope: Ethics Odd and Crucial." In *The Annual Society of Christian Ethics.* D.M. Yeager, ed. Washington: Georgetown Univ. Pp. 73-92.

——. 1990. "When Israel Gloats Over Shiloh." *Sojourners* 19:24-7.

——. (forthcoming) "Solomon as Patron of Wisdom." In *The Sage in Ancient Israel.* John Gammie and Leo G. Perdue, eds. Winona Lake: Eisenbrauns.

Buber, Martin. 1946. *Moses.* Atlantic Highlands, NJ: Humanities Press International.

——. 1967. *The Kingship of God.* New York: Harper & Row.

Campbell, A. F. 1979. "Psalm 78: A Contribution to the Theology of Tenth Century Israel." *CBQ* 41:51-79.

Clifford, Richard J. 1981. "In Zion and David a New Beginning: An Interpretation of Psalm 78." In *Traditions in Transformation.* Baruch Halpern and Jon D. Levenson, eds. Winona Lake: Eisenbrauns. Pp. 121-41.

Cohen, Martin A. 1965. "The Role of the Shilonite Priesthood in the United Monarchy of Ancient Israel." *Hebrew Union College Annual* 36:59-98.

Connenton, Paul. 1980. *The Tragedy of Enlightenment: An Essay on the Frankfurt School.* Cambridge: Cambridge Univ.

Coote, Robert B. and Keith W. Whitelam. 1987. *The Emergence of Early Israel in Historical Perspective.* The Social World of Biblical Antiquity Series 5. Sheffield: Almond.

Crenshaw, James L. 1984. *Whirlpool of Torment.* Philadelphia: Fortress.

Day, Peggy L., ed. 1989. *Gender and Difference in Ancient Israel.* Minneapolis: Fortress.

Doll, Peter. 1985. *Menschenschöpfung und Weltschöpfung in der alttestamentliche Weisheit.* Stuttgart Bibel Studien 117. Stuttgart: Verlag Katholisches Bibelwerk.

Engelbert, Jo Anne. 1988. "Introduction." In *And We Sold the Rain.* Rosono Santos, ed. New York: Four Walls Eight Windows.

Fackenheim, Émil. 1970. *God's Presence in History.* New York: New York Univ.

Fisch, Harold. 1988. *Poetry with a Purpose: Biblical Poetics and Interpretation.* Bloomington: Indiana Univ.

Fishbane, Michael. 1979. *Text and Texture.* Boston: Schocken.

Fox-Genovese, Elizabeth. 1982. "Placing Women's History in History." *New Left Review* 133 (May/June): 5-29.

Gallie, W. B. 1964. *Philosophy and the Historical Understanding.* London: Chatto & Windus.

Ganaway, George K. 1989. "Exploring the Credibility Issue in Multiple Personality Disorder and Related Dissociative Phenomena." Presented to the Fourth Regional Conference on Multiple Personality and Dissociative States, April 8.

Garbini, Giovanni. 1988. *History and Ideology in Ancient Israel.* New York: Crossroad.

Gerstenberger, Erhard. 1971. "Der klagende Mensch." In *Probleme biblischer Theologie.* Hans Walter Wolff, ed. Munich: Chr. Kaiser. Pp. 64-72.

———. 1974. "The Psalms." In *Old Testament Form Criticism.* John H. Hayes, ed. San Antonio: Trinity Univ. Pp. 212-4.

Gilbert, Sandra M. and Susan Gubar. 1979. *The Madwoman in the Attic.* New Haven: Yale Univ.

Gilkey, Langdon. 1961. "Cosmology, Ontology and the Travail of Biblical Language." *Journal of Religion* 41:194-205.

Goldingay, John. 1981. "The Dynamic Cycle of Praise and Prayer in the Psalms." *JSOT* 20:85-90.

Gordimer, Nadine. 1987. *A Sport of Nature.* New York: Knopf.

Gossman, Lionel. 1978. *The Writing of History.* Robert H. Canary and Henry Kozicki, eds. Madison: Univ. of Wisconsin.

Gottwald, Norman K. 1979. *The Tribes of Yahweh.* Maryknoll: Orbis.

Green, Garrett. 1989. *Imagining God: Theology and the Religious Imagination.* San Francisco: Harper & Row.

Green, Gayle and Coppela Kahn, eds. 1985. *Making a Difference: Feminist Literary Criticism.* London: Methuen.

Gutierrez, Gustavo. 1987. *On Job.* Maryknoll: Orbis.

Haley, Alex. 1976. *Roots.* Garden City: Doubleday.

Hallo, William W. 1980. "Biblical History in its Near Eastern Setting." In *Scripture in Context.* Carl D. Evans et al, eds. Pittsburgh: Pickwick.

Halpern, Baruch. 1988. *The First Historians: The Hebrew Bible and History.* San Francisco: Harper & Row.

Hardy, Daniel N. and David F. Ford. 1985. *Praising and Knowing God.* Philadelphia: Westminster.

Harrelson, Walter. 1977. "Life, Faith, and the Emergence of Tradition." *Tradition and Theology in the Old Testament.* Douglas A. Knight, ed. Philadelphia: Fortress. Pp. 11-30.

Hartman, Goeffrey H. 1981. *Saving the Text: Literature, Derrida, Philosophy.* Baltimore: Johns Hopkins Univ.

Harvey, Van A. 1981. *The Historian and the Believer: The Morality of Historical Knowledge and Christian Belief.* Philadelphia: Westminster.

Hayes, John H. and J. Maxwell Miller. 1977. *Israelite and Judean History.* London: SCM.

Herion, Gary A. 1981. "The Role of Historical Narrative in Biblical Thought: The Tendencies Underlying Old Testament Historiography." *JSOT* 21:25-57.

Heschel, Abraham J. 1965. *Who Is Man?* Stanford: Stanford Univ.

Horkheimer, Max and T.W. Adorno. 1972. *Dialectic of Enlightenment*. New York: Herder.

Husserl, Edmund. 1986. "Essential Distinctions." In *The Hermeneutics Reader*. K. Mueller-Vollmer, ed. Oxford: Blackwell. Pp.166-77.

Joyce, Paul. 1989. *Divine Initiative and Human Response in Ezekiel*. JSOT Supplements 51. Sheffield: JSOT.

Kaufman, Gordon P. 1968. "On the Memory of 'Act of God'." *Harvard Theological Review* 61:175-201.

Kleinman, A. 1988. *The Illness Narratives*. New York: Basic Books.

Koch, Klaus. 1983. "Is there a Doctrine of Retribution in the Old Testament?" In *Theodicy in the Old Testament*. James L. Crenshaw, ed. Philadelphia: Fortress. Pp. 57-87.

Kolodny, Annette. 1985. "Dancing Through the Minefield" and "A Map of Reading." In *The New Feminist Criticism*. Elaine Showalter, ed. London: Virago. Pp. 46-62.

Lemke, Werner E. 1982. "Revelation through History in Recent Biblical Theology." *Interpretation* 36:34-46.

Lerner, Gerda. 1986. *The Creation of Patriarchy*. New York: Oxford Univ.

Lindbeck, George A. 1984. *The Nature of Doctrine: Religion and Theology in a Postliberal Age*. Philadelphia: Westminster.

Long, Burke O. 1982. "The Social World of Ancient Israel." *Interpretation* 36:243-55.

MacIntyre, Alasdair. 1988. *Whose Justice? Which Rationality?* Notre Dame: Univ. of Notre Dame.

Mays, James L. 1969. "Worship, World, and Power." *Interpretation* 23:315-30.

McCarter, P. Kyle, Jr. 1980. *I Samuel*. Anchor Bible 8. Garden City, NY: Doubleday.

Meese, Elizabeth A. 1985. "Sexual Politics and Critical Judgment." In *After Strange Texts: The Role of Theory in the Study of Literature*. Gregory S. Jay and David L. Miller, eds. Tuscaloosa: Univ. of Alabama. Pp. 85-100.

Mendenhall, George. 1955. *Law and Covenant in Israel and the Ancient Near East*. Pittsburgh: The Biblical Colloquium.

———. 1973. *The Tenth Generation*. Baltimore: Johns Hopkins Univ.

———. 1975. "The Conflict Between Value Systems and Social Control." In *Unity and Diversity*. Hans Goedicke and J.J.M. Roberts, eds. Baltimore: Johns Hopkins Univ.

Michnich, Adam. 1985. *Letters from Prison and Other Essays*. Berkeley: Univ. of California.

Miller, J. Maxwell. 1985. "Israelite History." In *The Hebrew Bible and Its Modern Interpreters*. Douglas A. Knight and Gene M. Tucker, eds. Philadelphia: Fortress. Pp. 1-30.

Mitchell, W. J. T. 1986. *Iconology: Image, Text, Ideology*. Chicago: Univ. of Chicago.

Moberly, R. Walter L. 1983. *At the Mountain of God*. JSOT Supplements 22. Sheffield: JSOT.

O'Day, Gail R. 1986. *Revelation in the Fourth Gospel: Narrative Mode and Theological Claim*. Philadelphia: Fortress.

Odin, Thomas. 1984. *Care of Souls in the Classic Tradition*. Philadelphia: Fortress.

Ozick, Cynthia. 1989. *Metaphor and Memory*. New York: Alfred A. Knopp.

Polzin, Robert. 1980. *Moses and the Deuteronomist: A Literary Study of the Deuteronomic History*. New York: Seabury.

———. 1989. *Samuel and the Deuteronomist: A Literary Study of the Deuteronomic History, 1 Samuel*. San Francisco: Harper & Row.

Redfield, Robert. 1967. "The Social Organization of Tradition." In *Peasant Society: A Reader*. J.M. Potter, ed. Boston: Little, Brown, & Co. Pp. 25-34.

Richardson, Alan. 1964. *History Sacred and Profane*. London: SCM.

Ricoeur, Paul. 1984. *The Reality of the Historical Past*. Milwaukee: Marquette Univ.

———. 1986. *Lectures on Ideology and Utopia*. New York: Columbia Univ.

Rorty, Richard. 1980. *Philosophy and the Mirror of Nature*. Oxford: Blackwell.

Schneidau, Herbert N. 1986. "Biblical Narrative and Modern Consciousness." In *The Bible and the Narrative Tradition*. Frank McConnell, ed. New York: Oxford Univ. Pp. 132-50.

———. 1987. "Let the Reader Understand." *Semeia* 39:133-45.

Schreiter, Robert J. 1985. *Constructing Local Theologies*. Maryknoll: Orbis.

Siraala, A. 1964. *The Voice of Illness*. Philadelphia: Fortress.

Smend, Rudolf. 1963. *Die Bundesformel*. Theologische Studien 68. Zurich: EVZ.

Soggin, J. Alberto. 1984. *A History of Israel*. London: SCM.

Spence, Donald P. 1982. *Narrative Truth and Historical Truth*. New York: W.W. Norton.

Steblin-Kamenskij, M. I. 1973. *The Saga Mind*. Odense: Odense Univ.

Steiner, George. 1989. *Real Presences: Is There Anything in What We Say?* London: Faber & Faber.

Theissen, Gerd. 1983. *Biblical Faith: An Evolutionary Approach*. Philadelphia: Fortress.

Thomas, Owen C., ed. 1983. *God's Activity in the World: The Contemporary Problem*. Chico: Scholars.

Thompson, John B. 1981. *Critical Hermeneutics: A Study in the Thought of Paul Ricoeur and Jurgen Habermas*. Cambridge: Cambridge Univ.

Thompson, Thomas L. 1974. *The Historicity of the Patriarchal Narratives*. Beihefte zur ZAW 133. Berlin: Walter de Gruyter.

Toulmin, Stephen. 1990. *Cosmopolis: The Hidden Agenda of Modernity*. New York: The Free Press.

Trible, Phyllis. 1984. *Texts of Terror: Literary Feminist Readings of Biblical Narratives*. Philadelphia: Fortress.

Van Buren, Paul. 1983. *A Theology of the Jewish-Christian Reality*, Vol. 2. San Francisco: Harper & Row.

van Iersel, Bas and Anton Weiler, eds. 1987. *Exodus—A Lasting Paradigm*. Edinburgh: T. & T. Clark.

van Seters, John. 1983. *In Search of History*. New Haven: Yale Univ.

Voegelin, Eric. 1956. *Order and History: Israel and Revelation*, Vol. 1. Baton Rouge: Louisiana State Univ.

——. 1956. *Israel and Revelation*. Baton Rouge: Louisiana State Univ.

von Rad, Gerhard. 1962. *Old Testament Theology*, Vol. 1. San Francisco: Harper & Row.

——. 1966. "The Form-Critical Problem of Hexateuch." In *The Problem of the Hexateuch and Other Essays*. New York: McGraw-Hill. Pp. 1-78.

Walzer, Michael. 1985. *Exodus and Revolution*. New York: Basic Books.

White, Hayden. 1973. *Metahistory: The Historical Imagination in Nineteenth Century Europe*. Baltimore: Johns Hopkins Univ.

——. 1978. "Rhetoric and History." In *Theories of History*. Hayden White and Frank E. Monuel, eds. Los Angeles: William Andrews Clark Memorial Library. Pp. 3-25.

——. 1978. "The Historical Text as Literary Artifact." In *The Writing of History: Literary Form and Historical Understanding*. Robert H. Canary and Henry Kozechi, eds. Madison: Univ. of Wisconsin. Pp. 44-61.

——. 1987. *The Content of the Form: Narrative Discourse and Historical Representation*. Baltimore: Johns Hopkins Univ.

Wilder, Amos. 1983. "Story and Story-World." *Interpretation* 37: 353-64.

Wiles, Maurice. 1986. *God's Action in the World*. London: SCM.

Wolff, Hans Walter. 1964. "'Wissen um Gott' bei Hosea als Urform von Theologie." In *Gesammelte Studien zum Alten Testament*. ThB 22. Munich: Chr. Kaiser.

Wolff, Virginia. 1929. *A Room to One's Own*. London: Hogarth.

Wright, G. Ernest. 1952. *God Who Acts*. SBT 8. London: SCM.

——. 1957. *Biblical Archaeology*. Philadelphia: Westminster.

Yerushalmi, Yosef Hayim. 1982. *Zakhor: Jewish History and Jewish Memory*. Seattle: Univ. of Washington.

Zikmund, Barbara Brown, ed. 1984. *Hidden Histories in the United Church of Christ*.

Zinn, Howard. 1980. *A People's History of the United States*. London: Longman.

INDEXES

AUTHORS

BIBLICAL REFERENCES